I0482482

Adult Coloring Book

In the Jungle

The Mighty Magic Jungle

100% Original Art

Mix Books, LLC
mix-booksonline.com

www.mix-booksonline.com/category/coloring-books

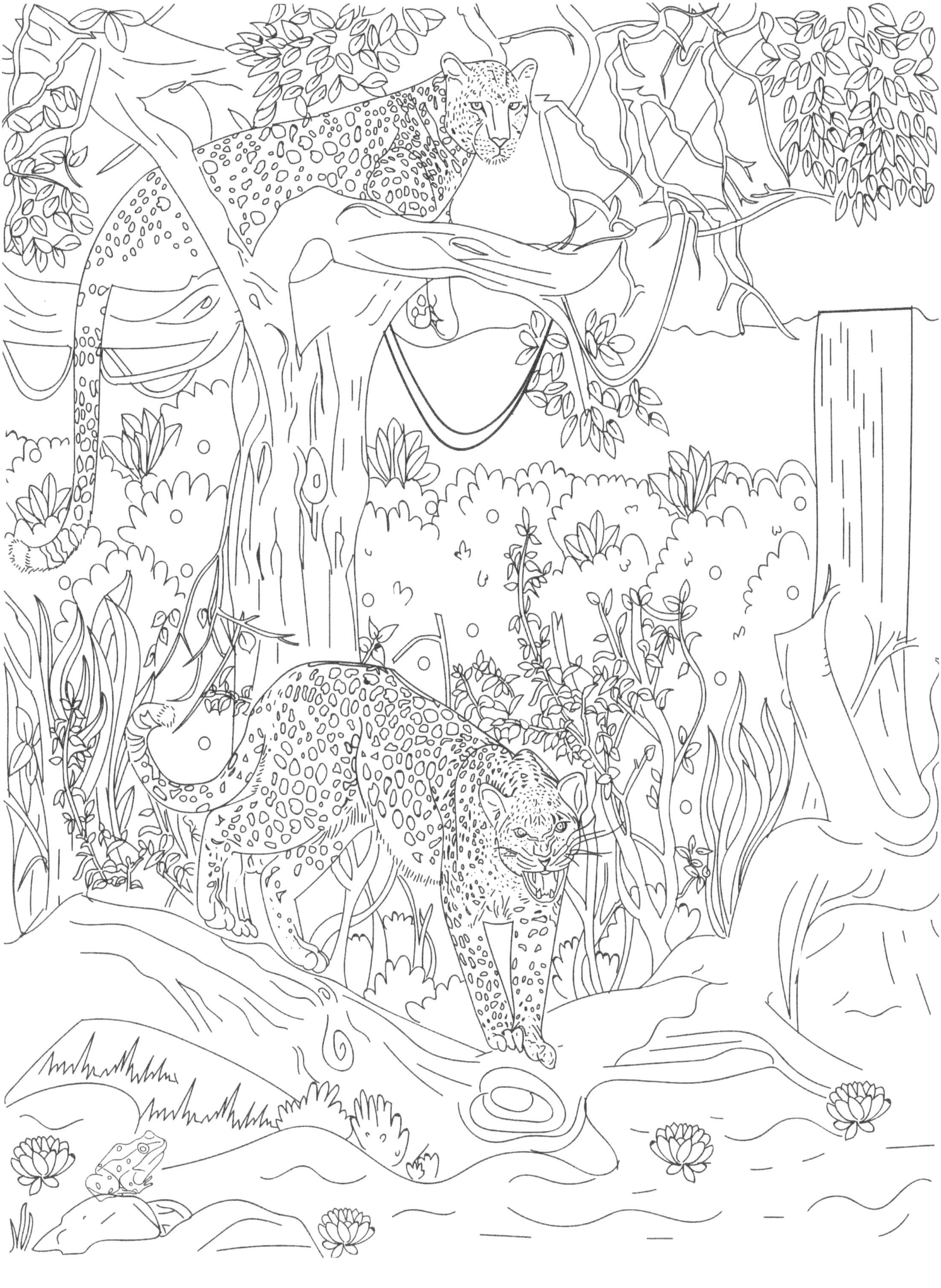

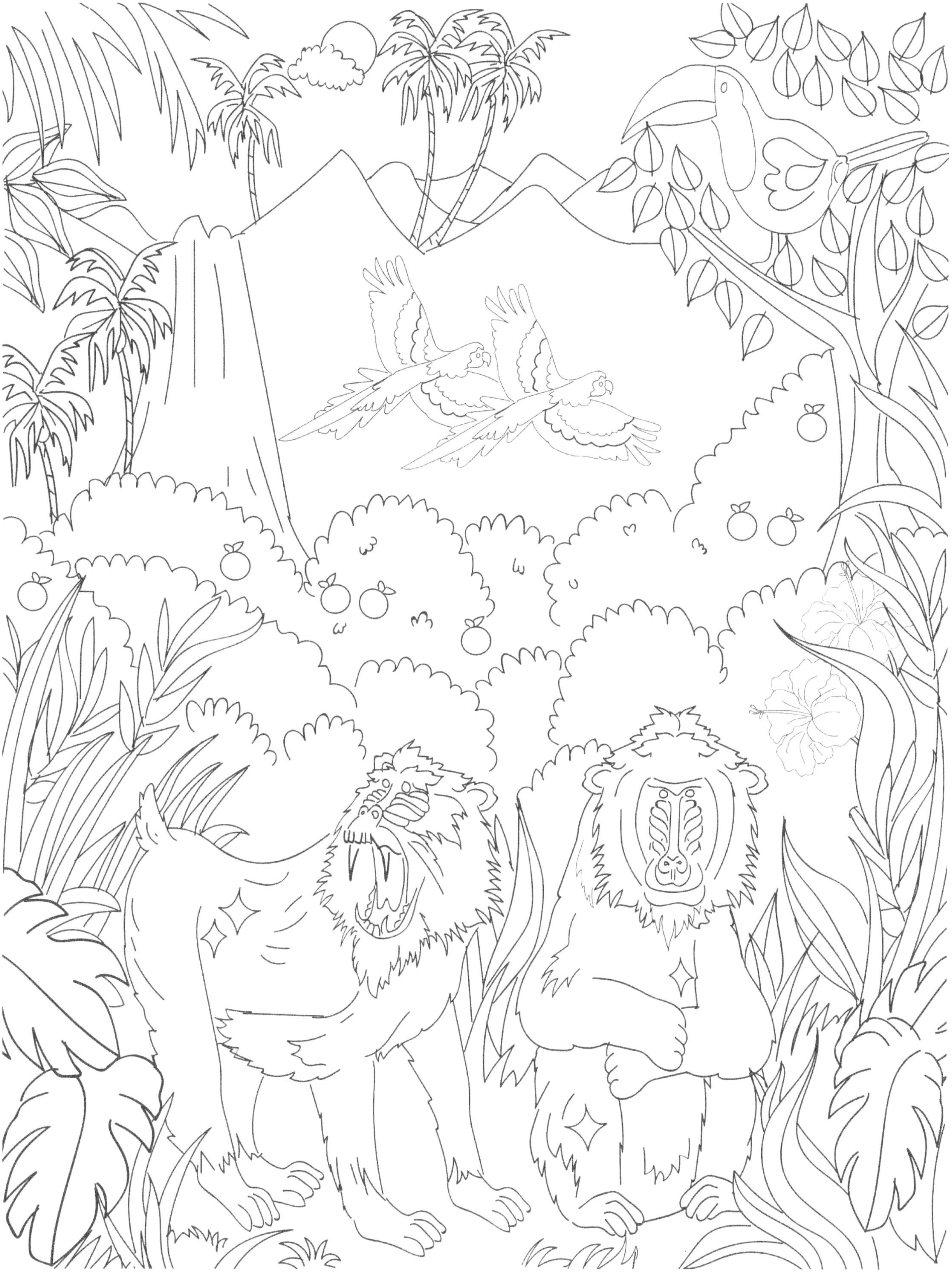

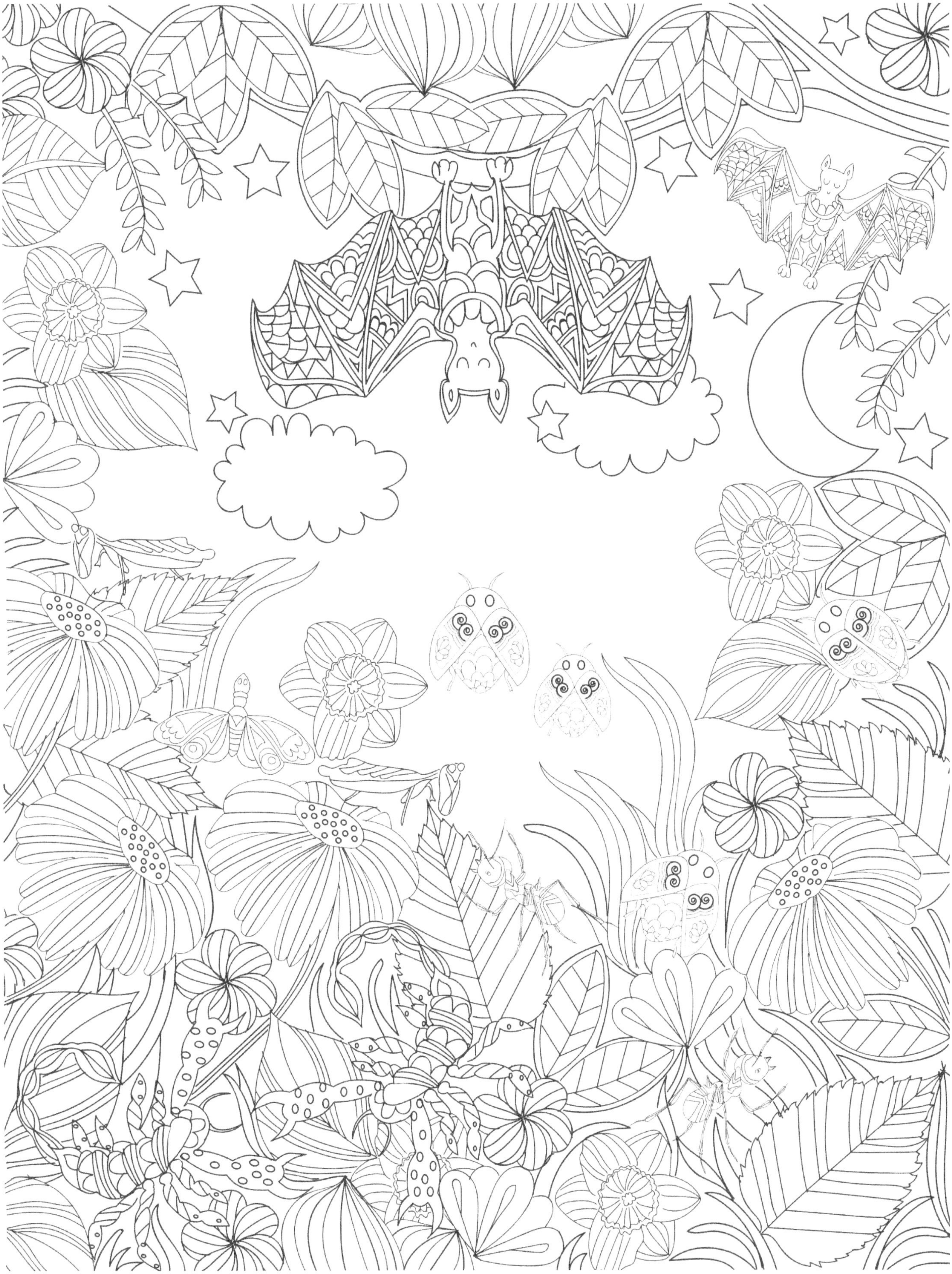

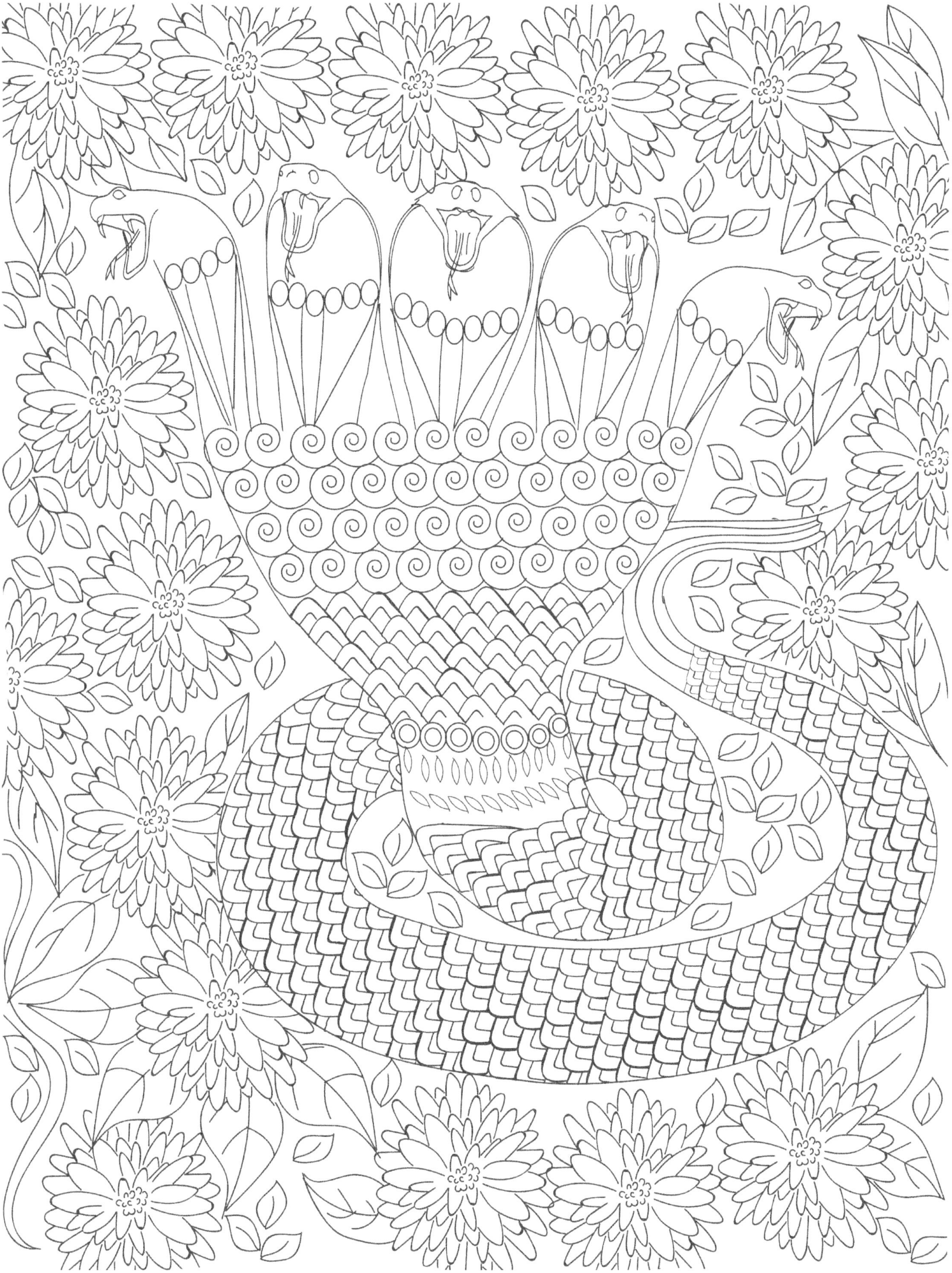

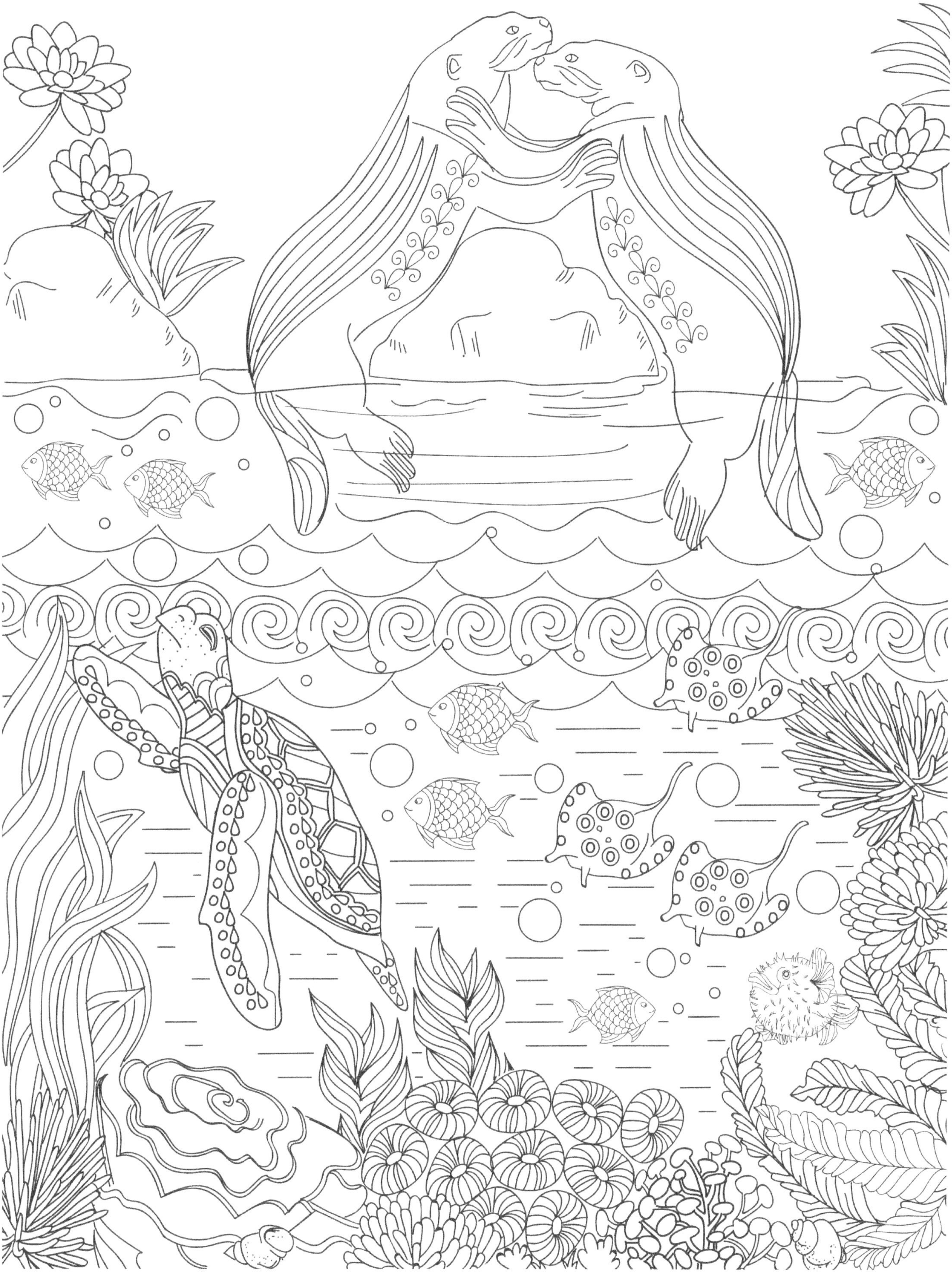

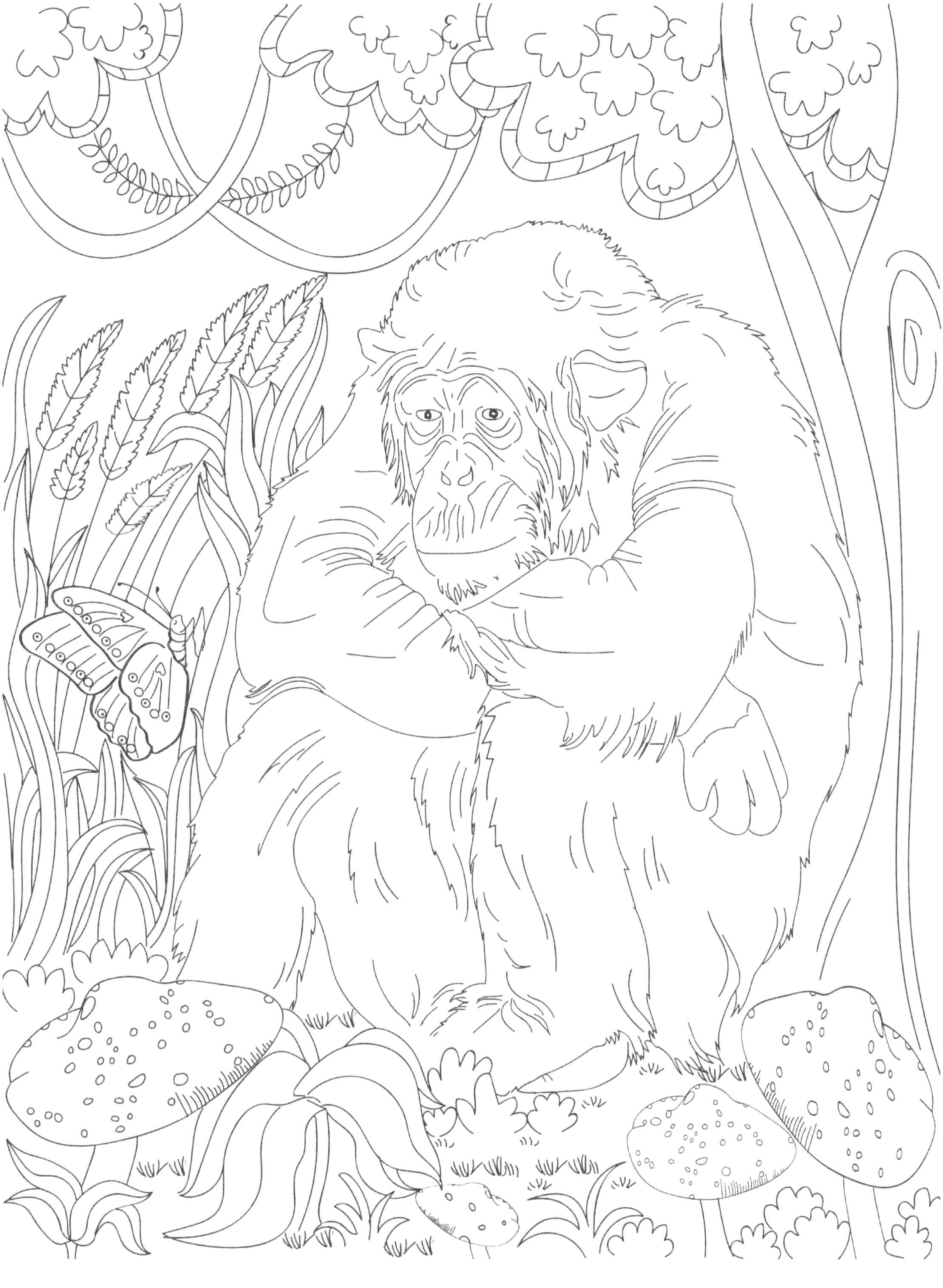

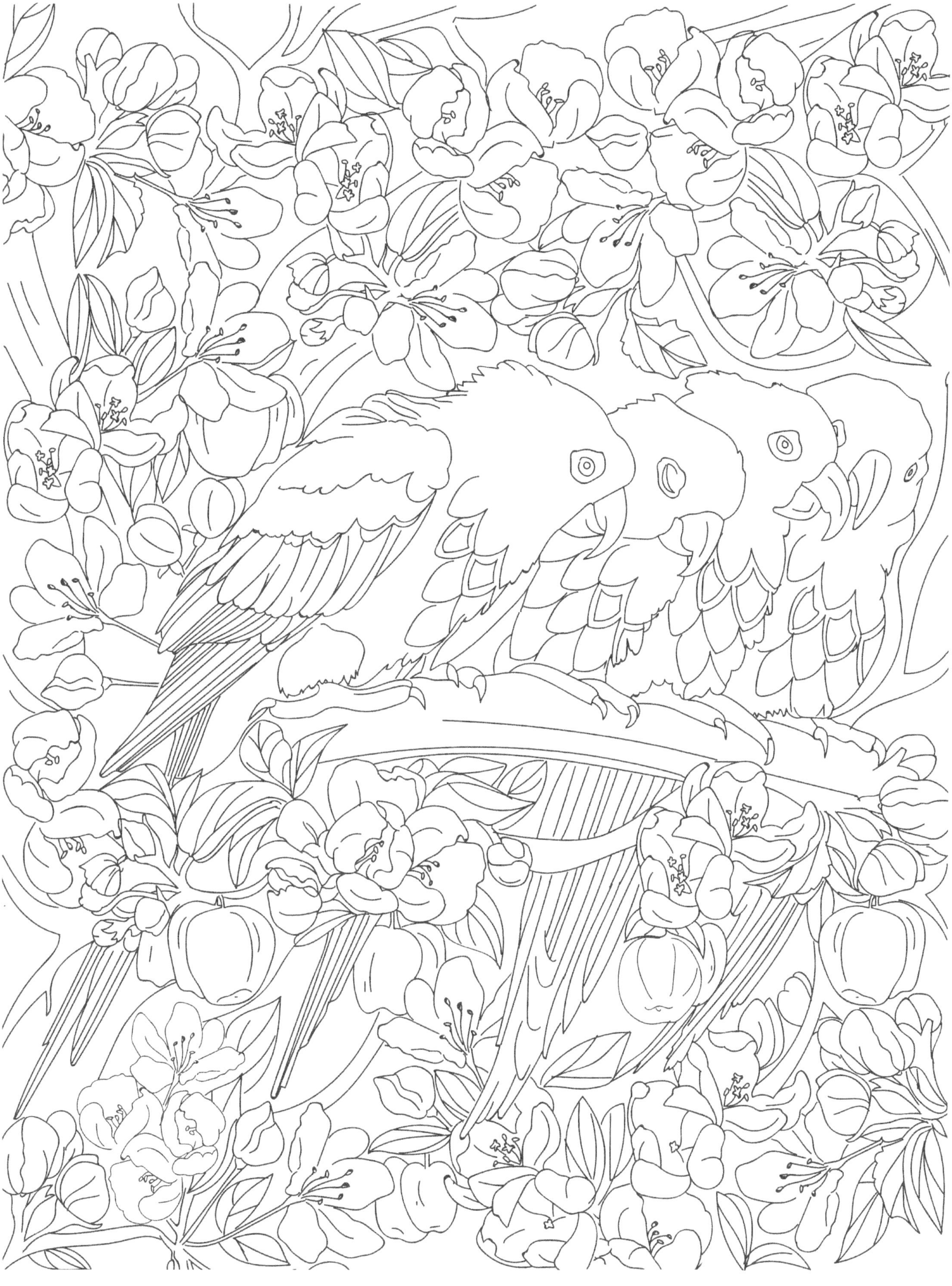

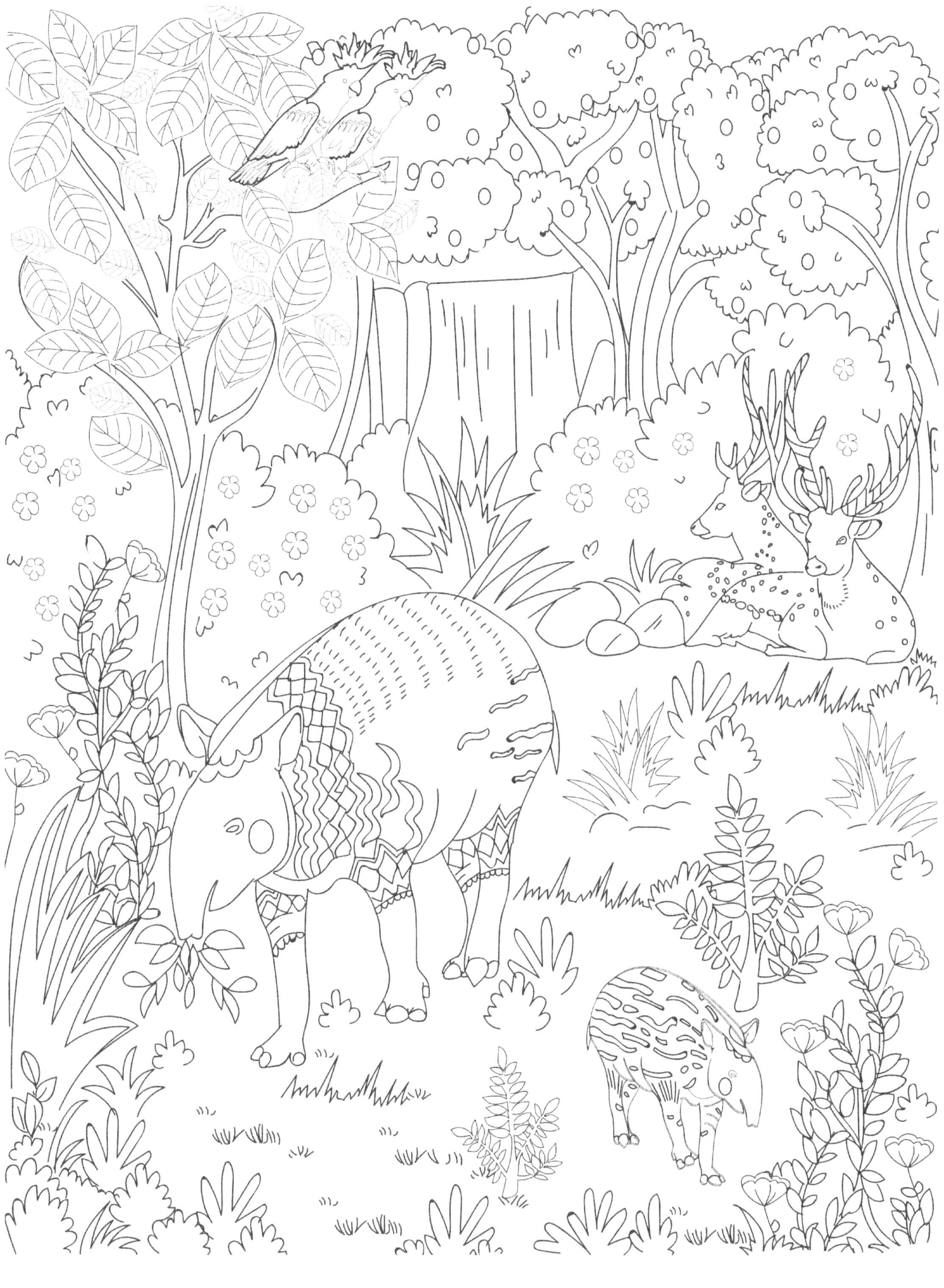

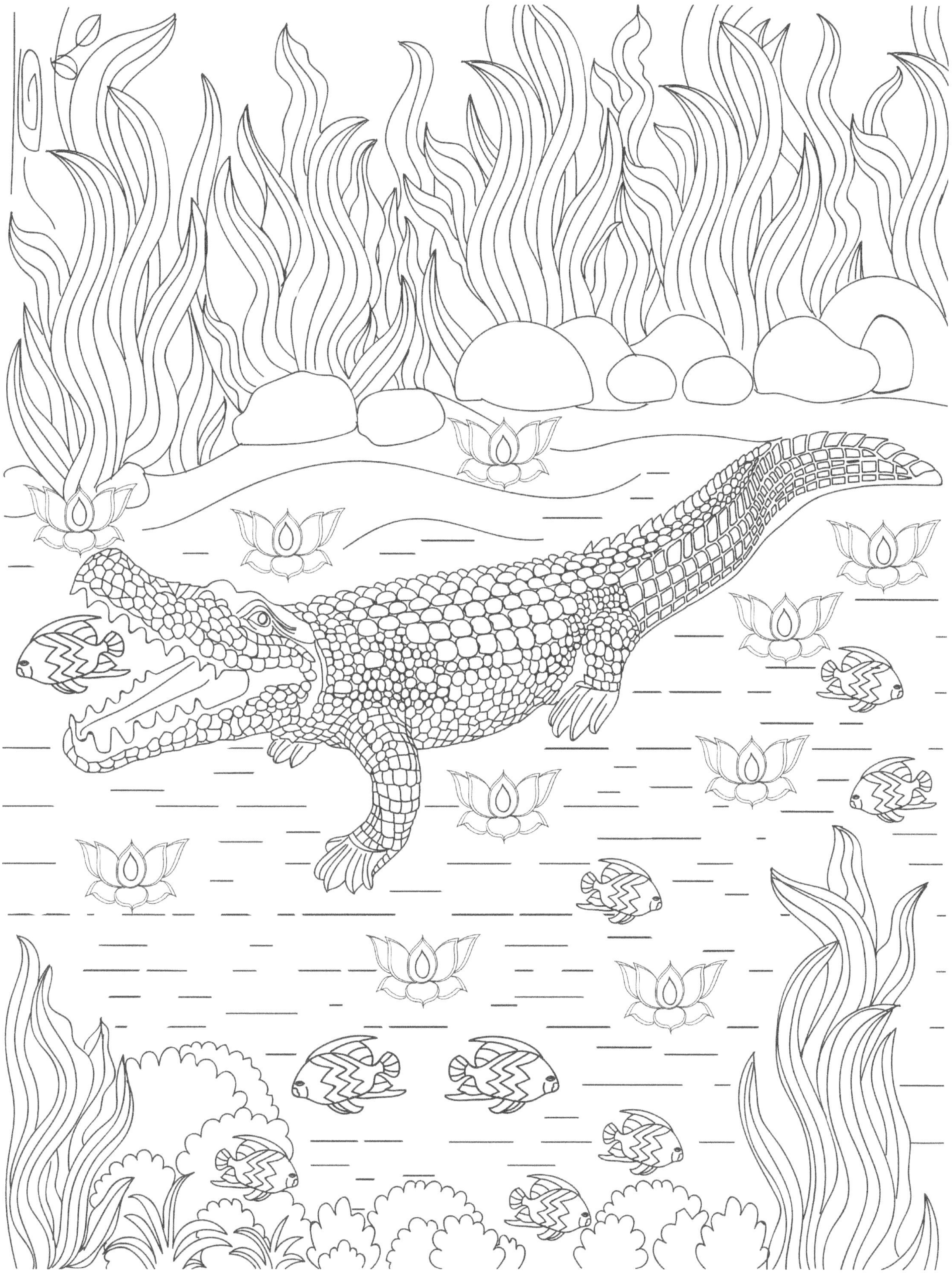

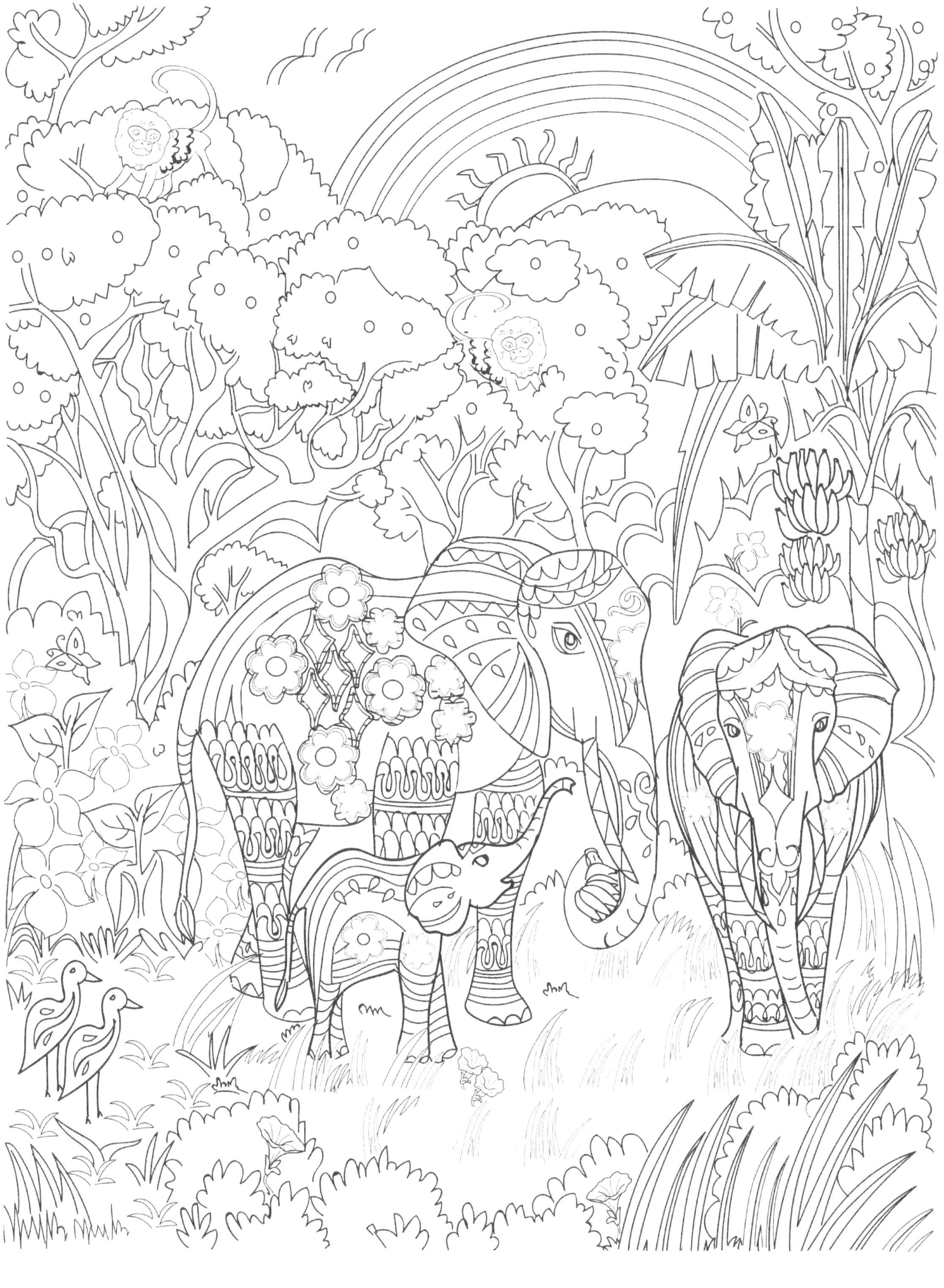

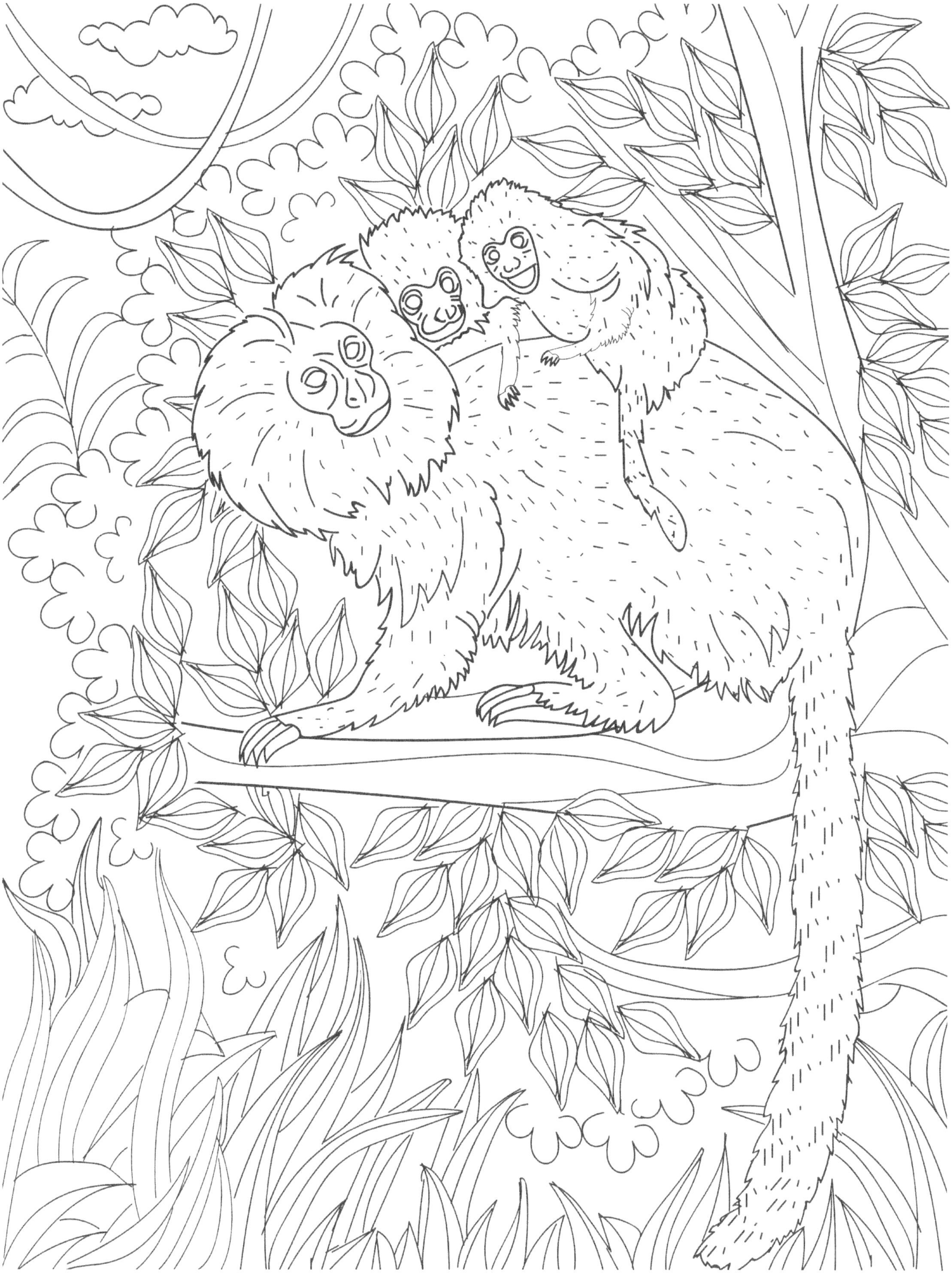

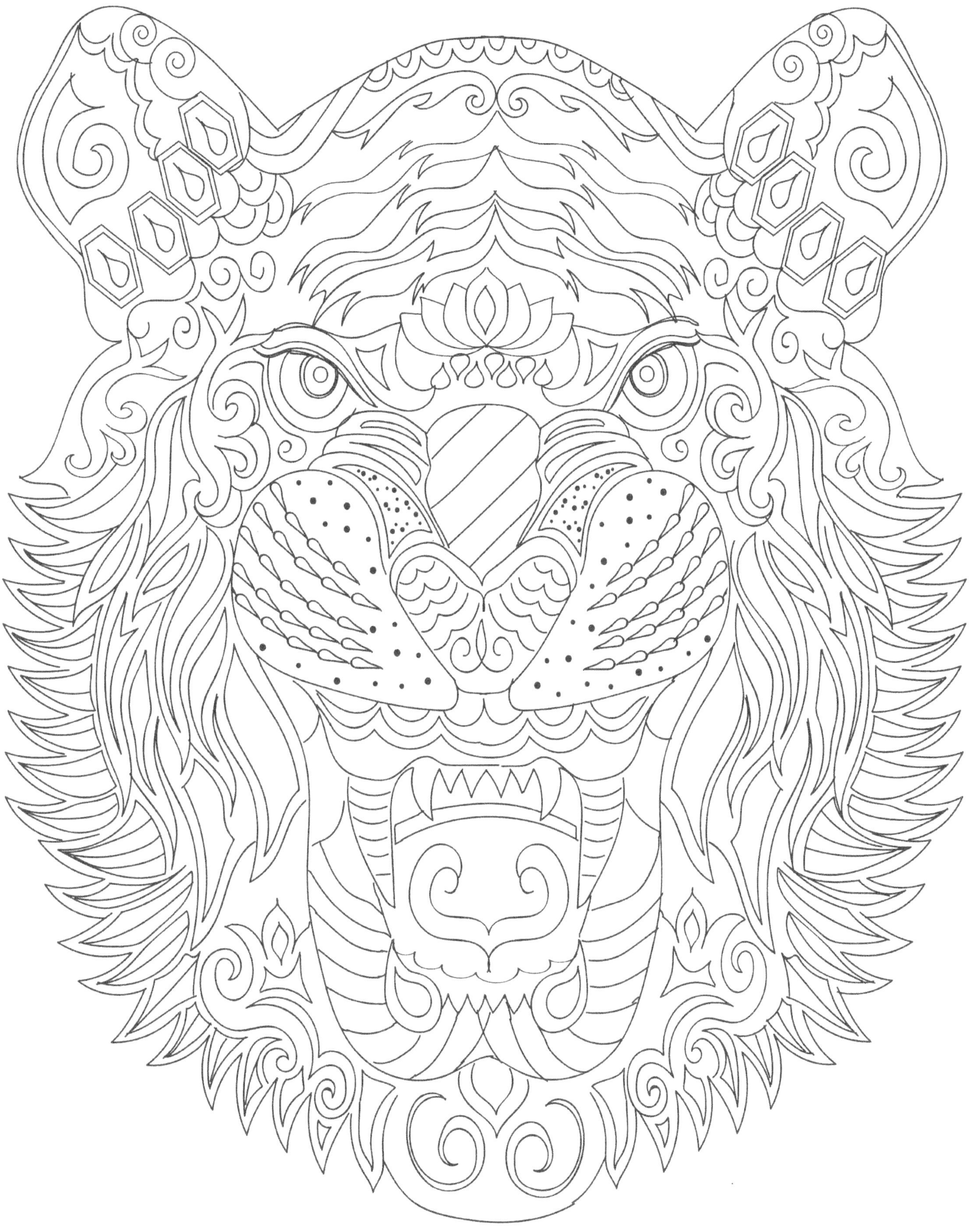

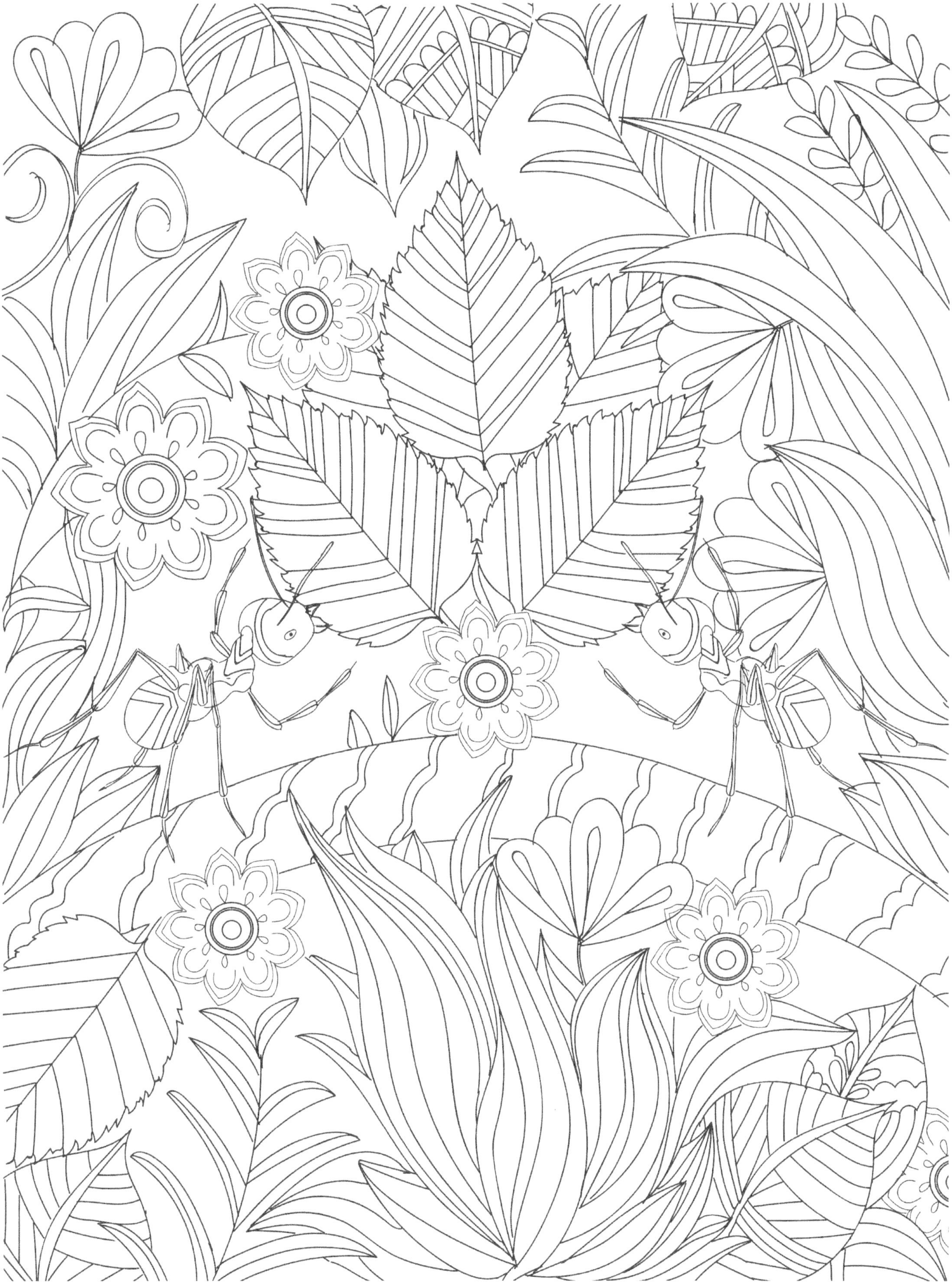

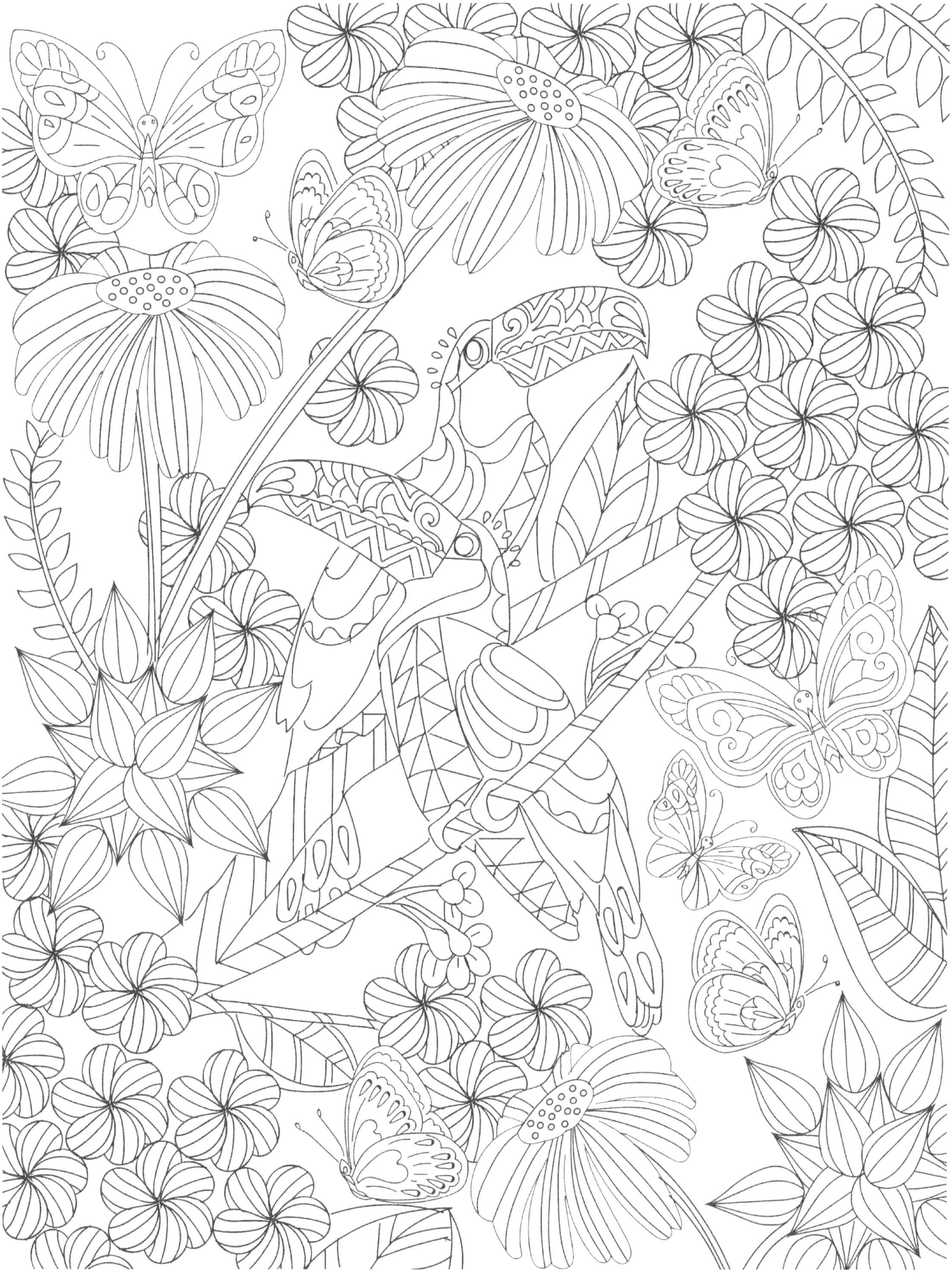

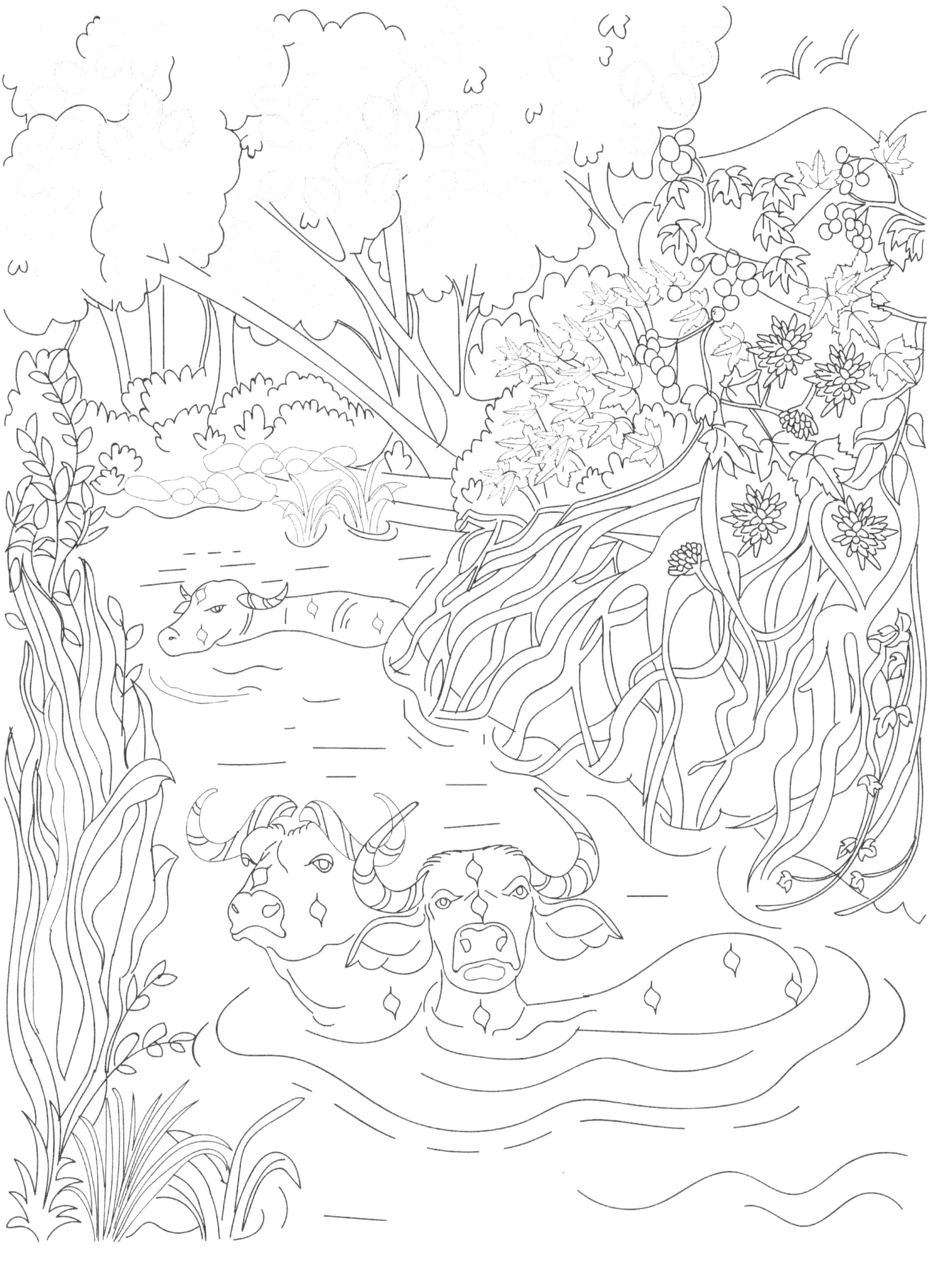

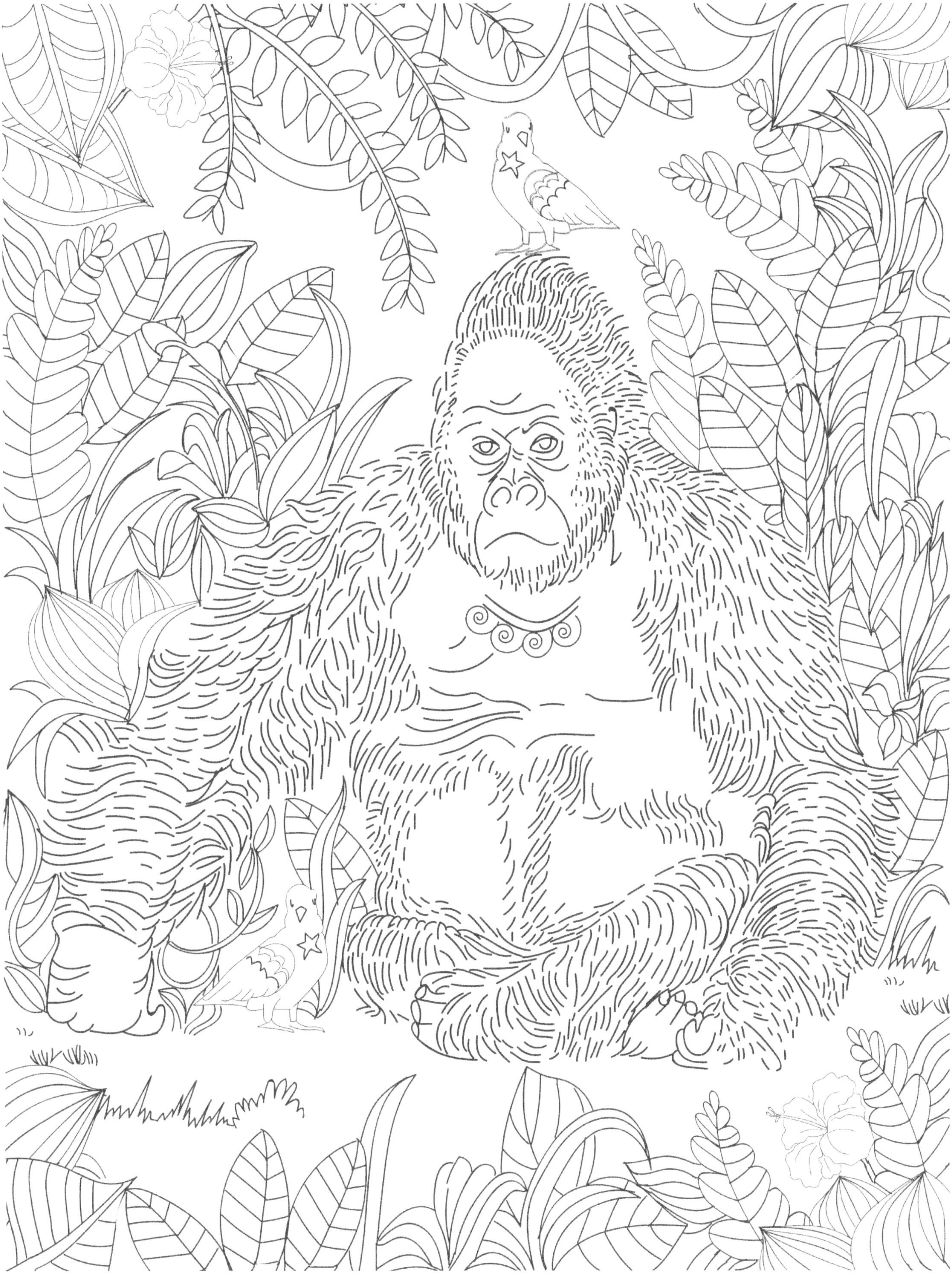

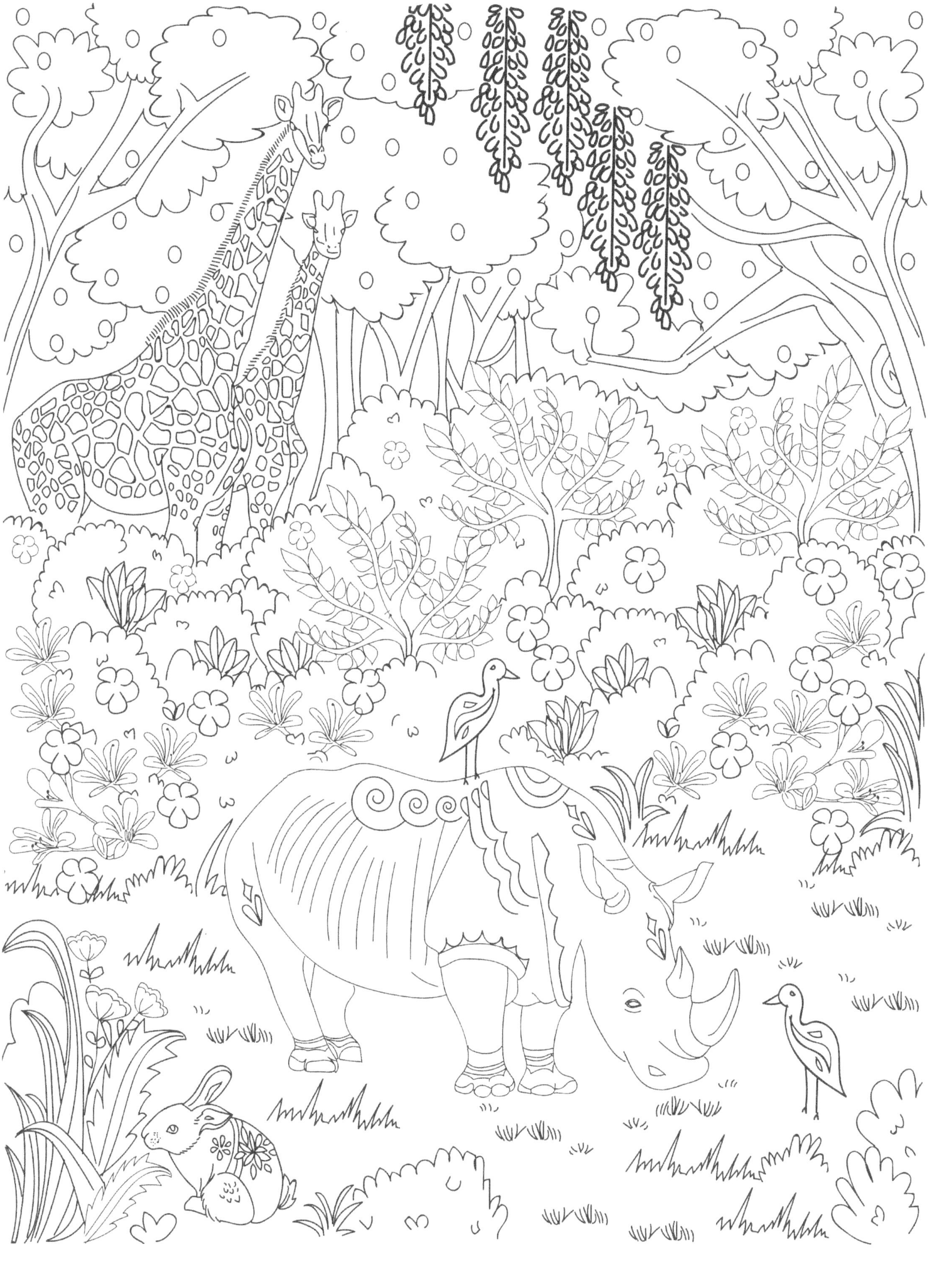

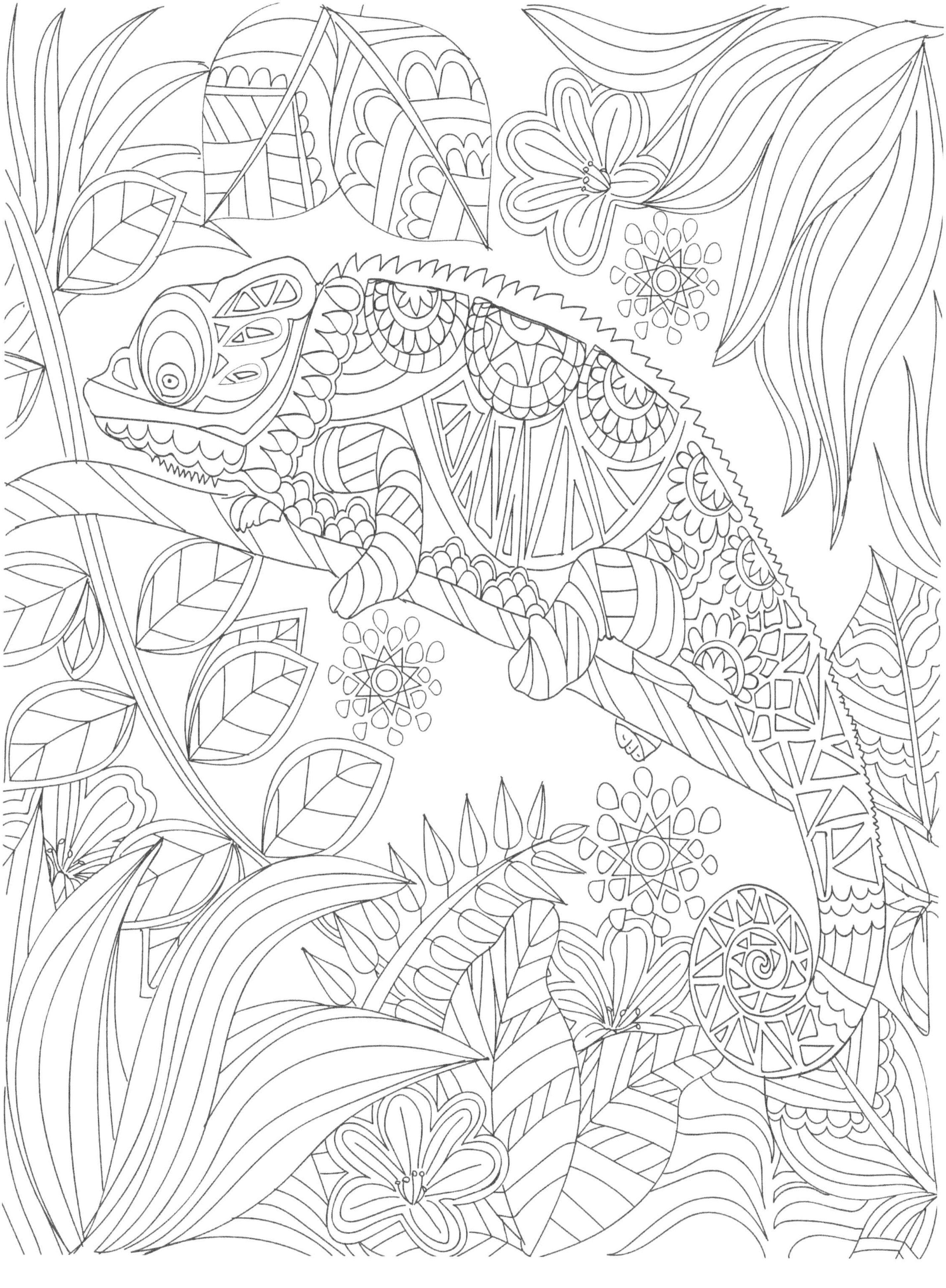

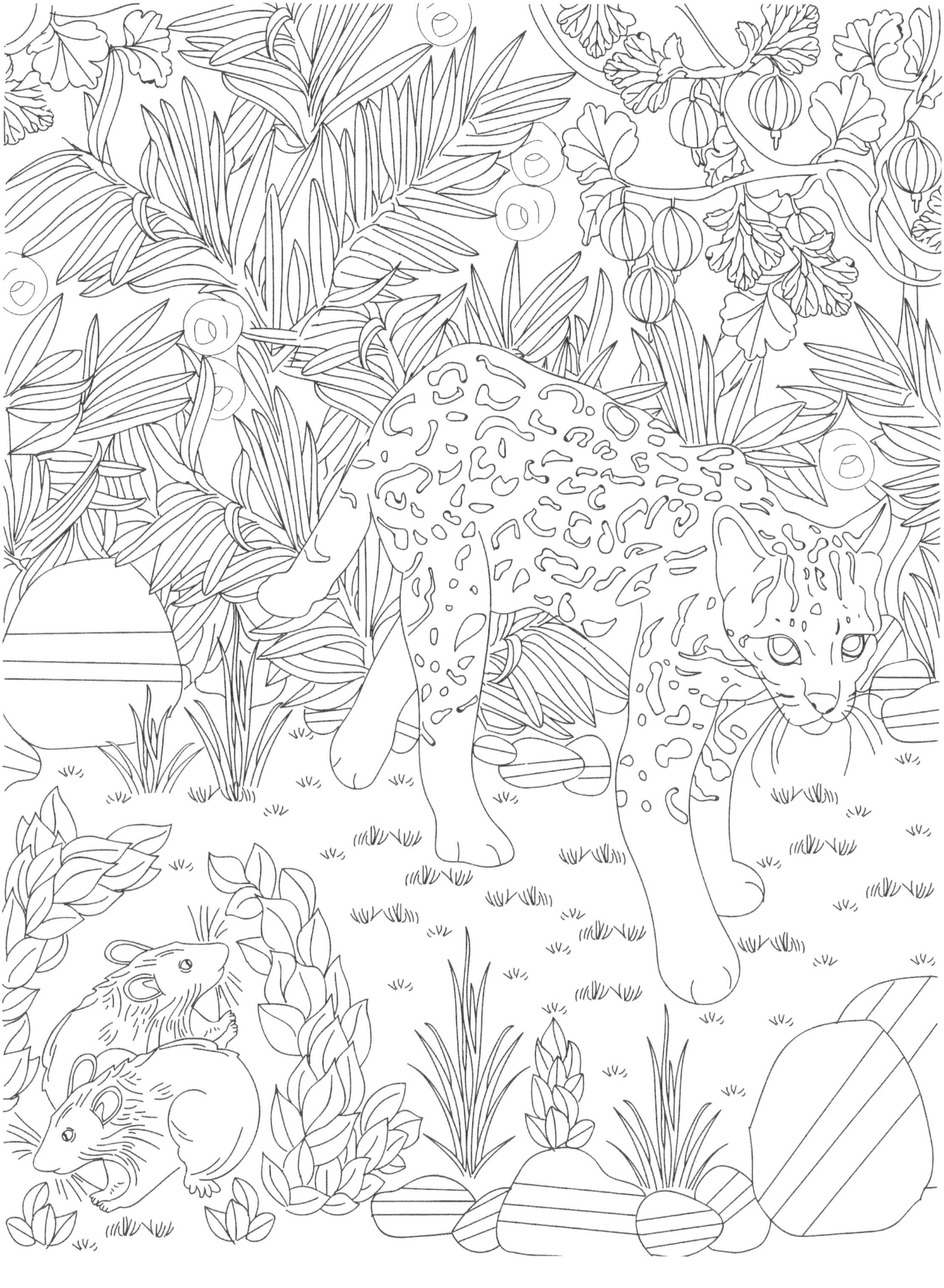

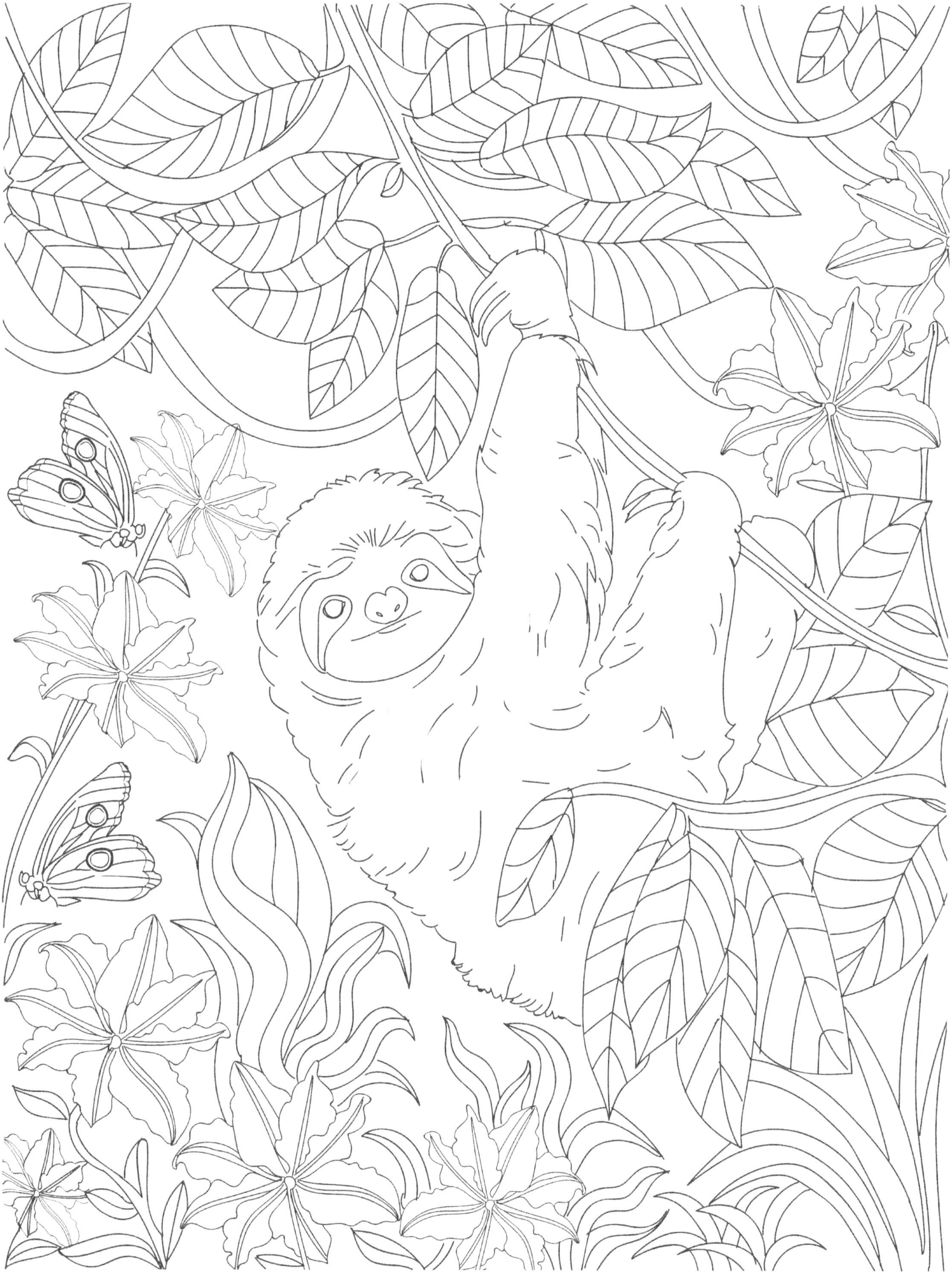

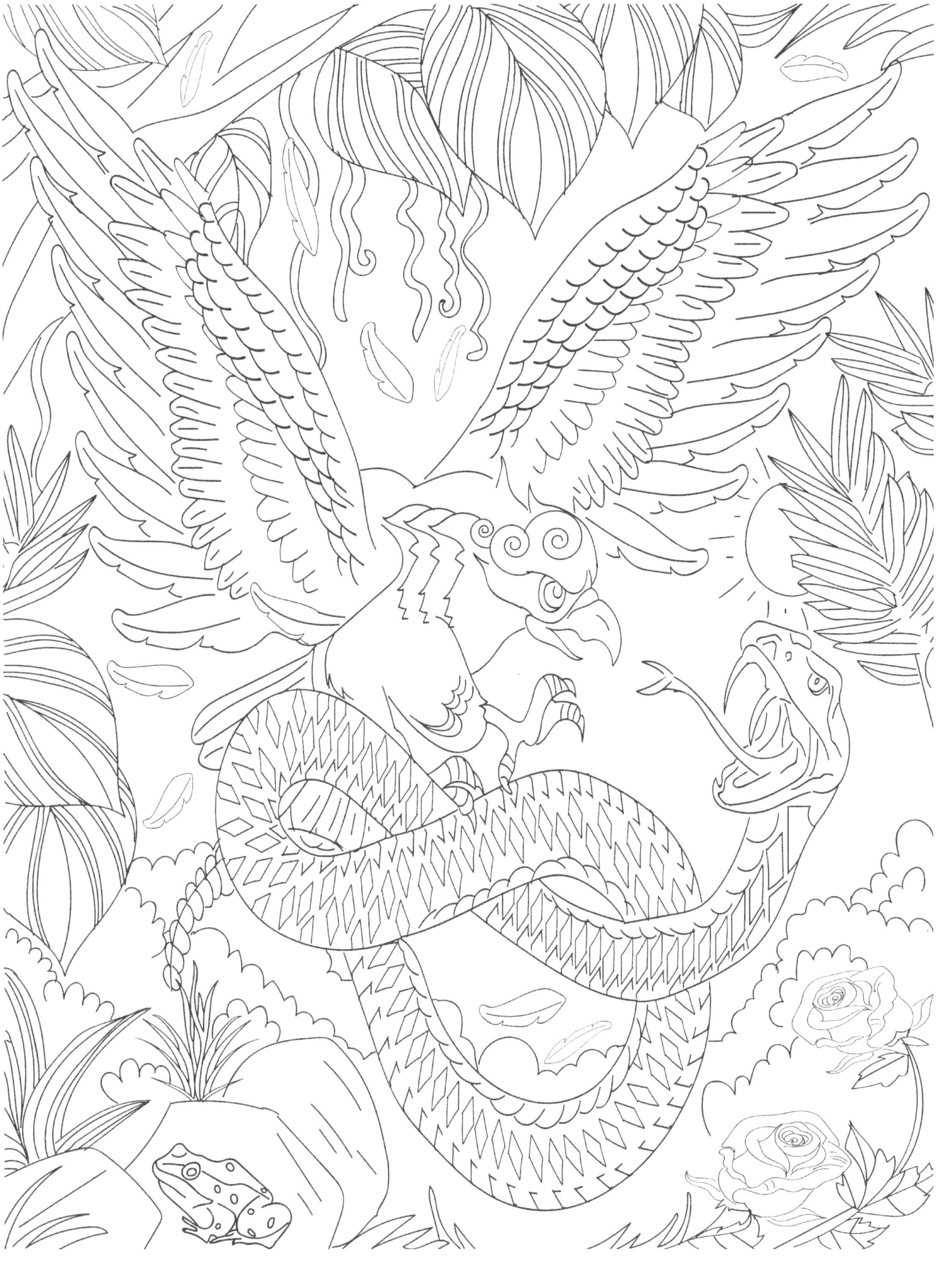

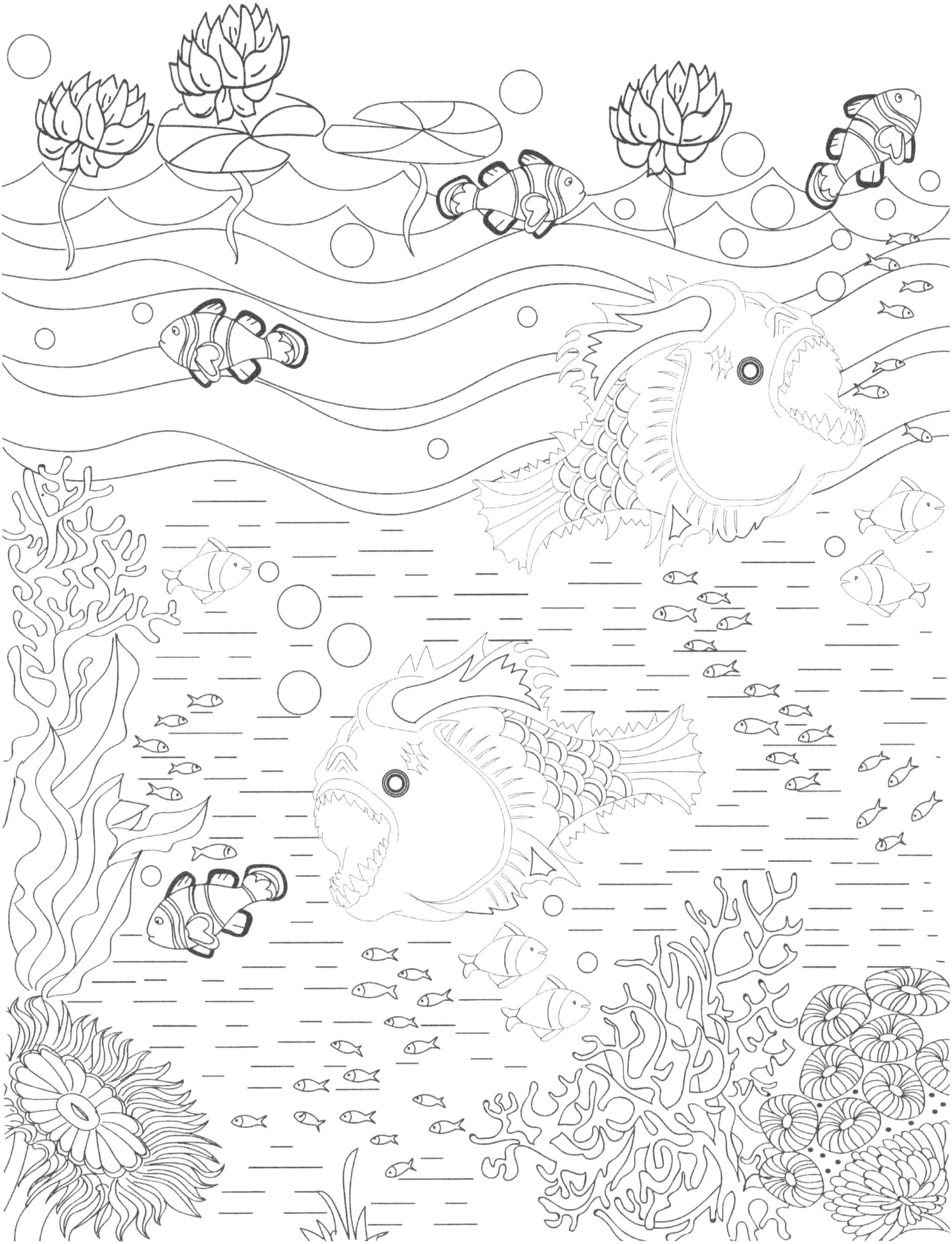

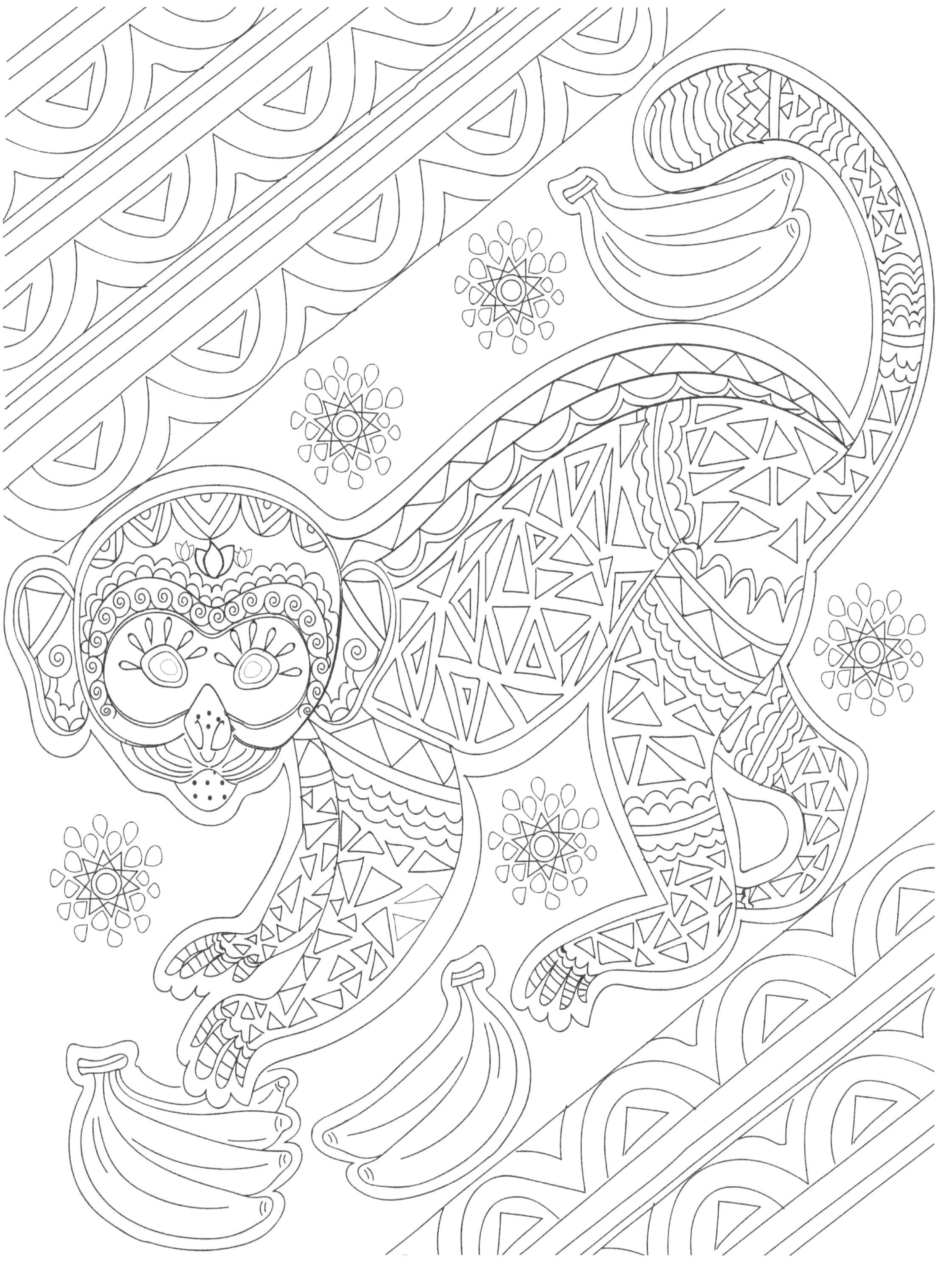

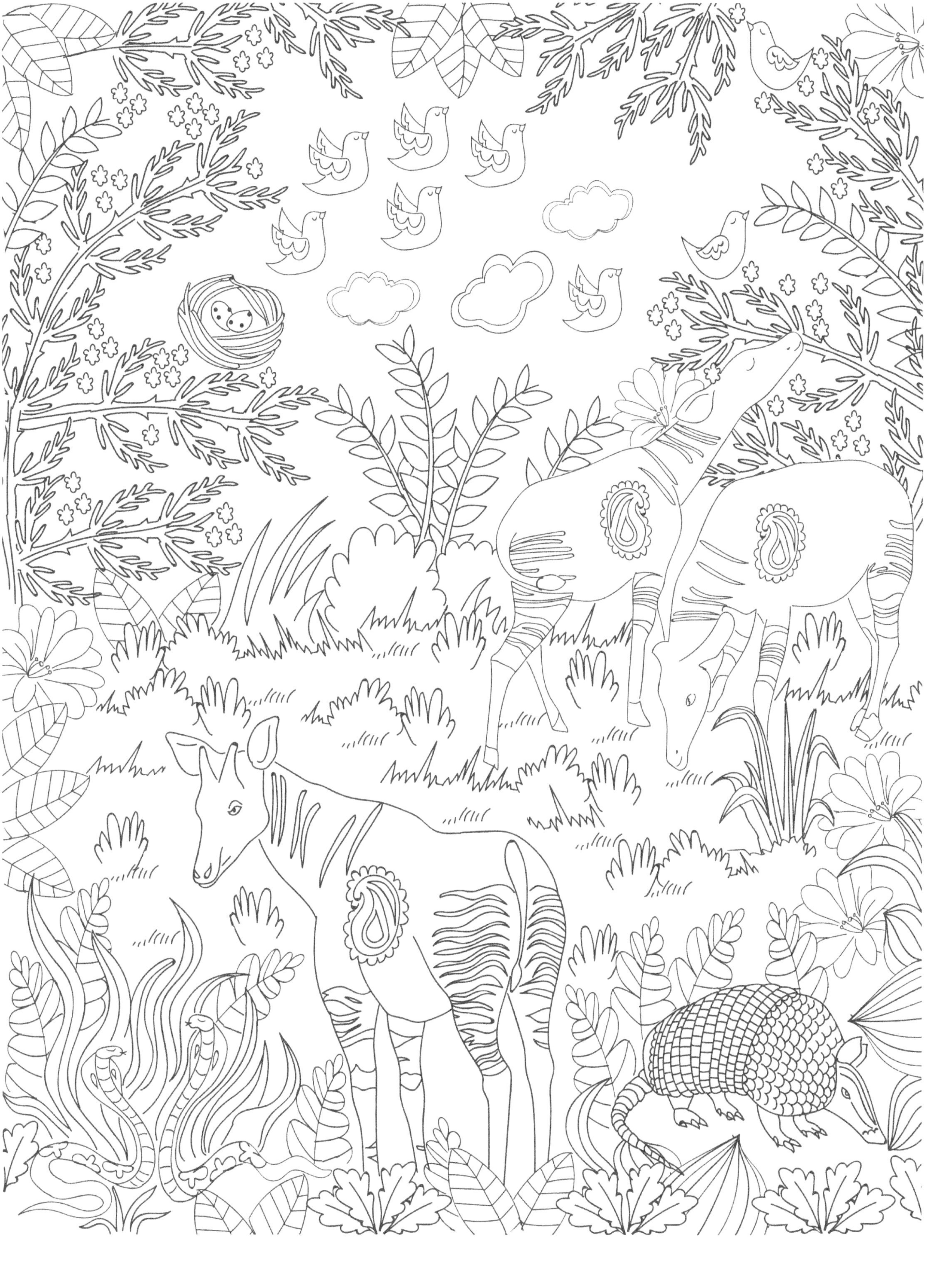

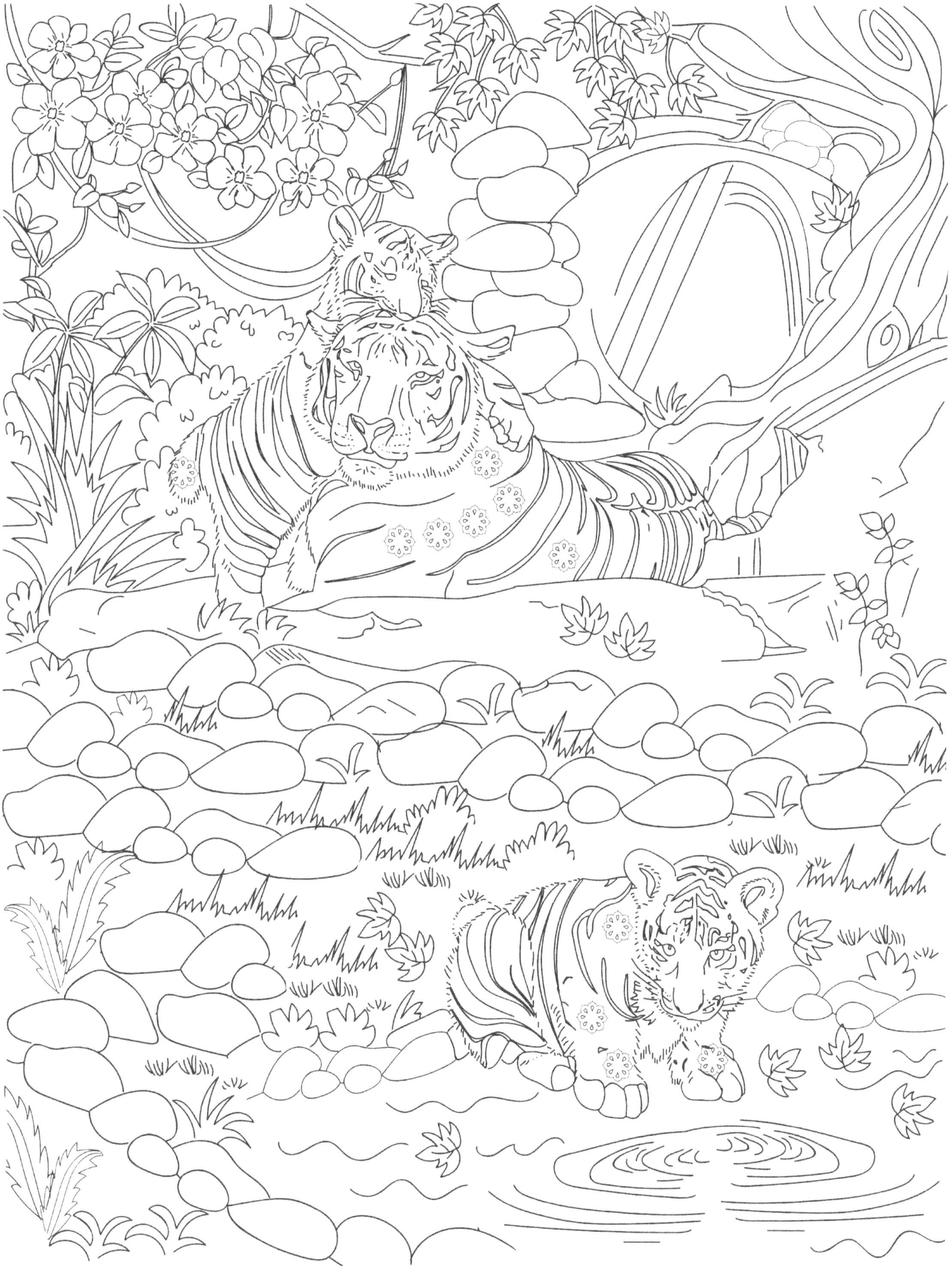

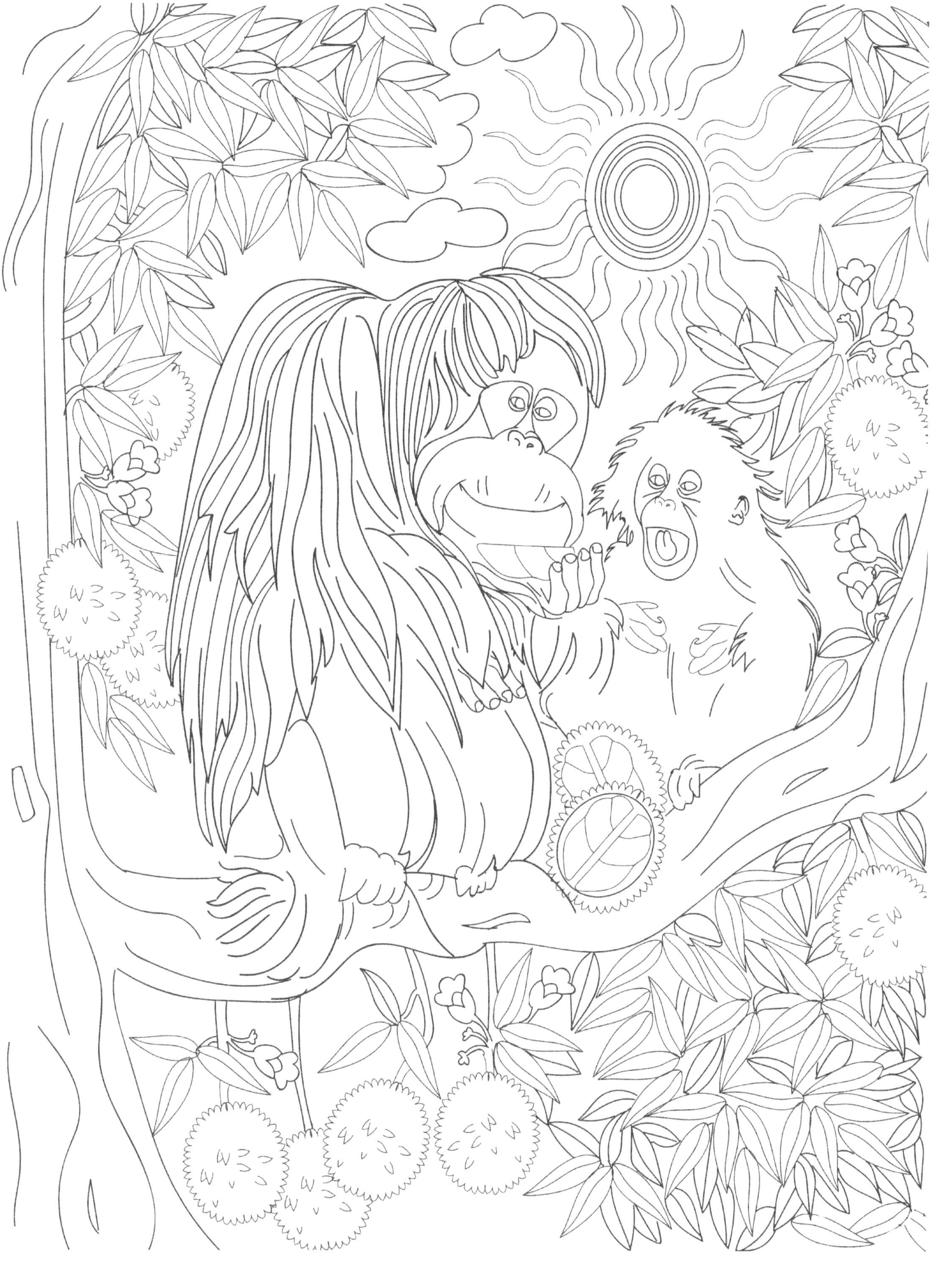

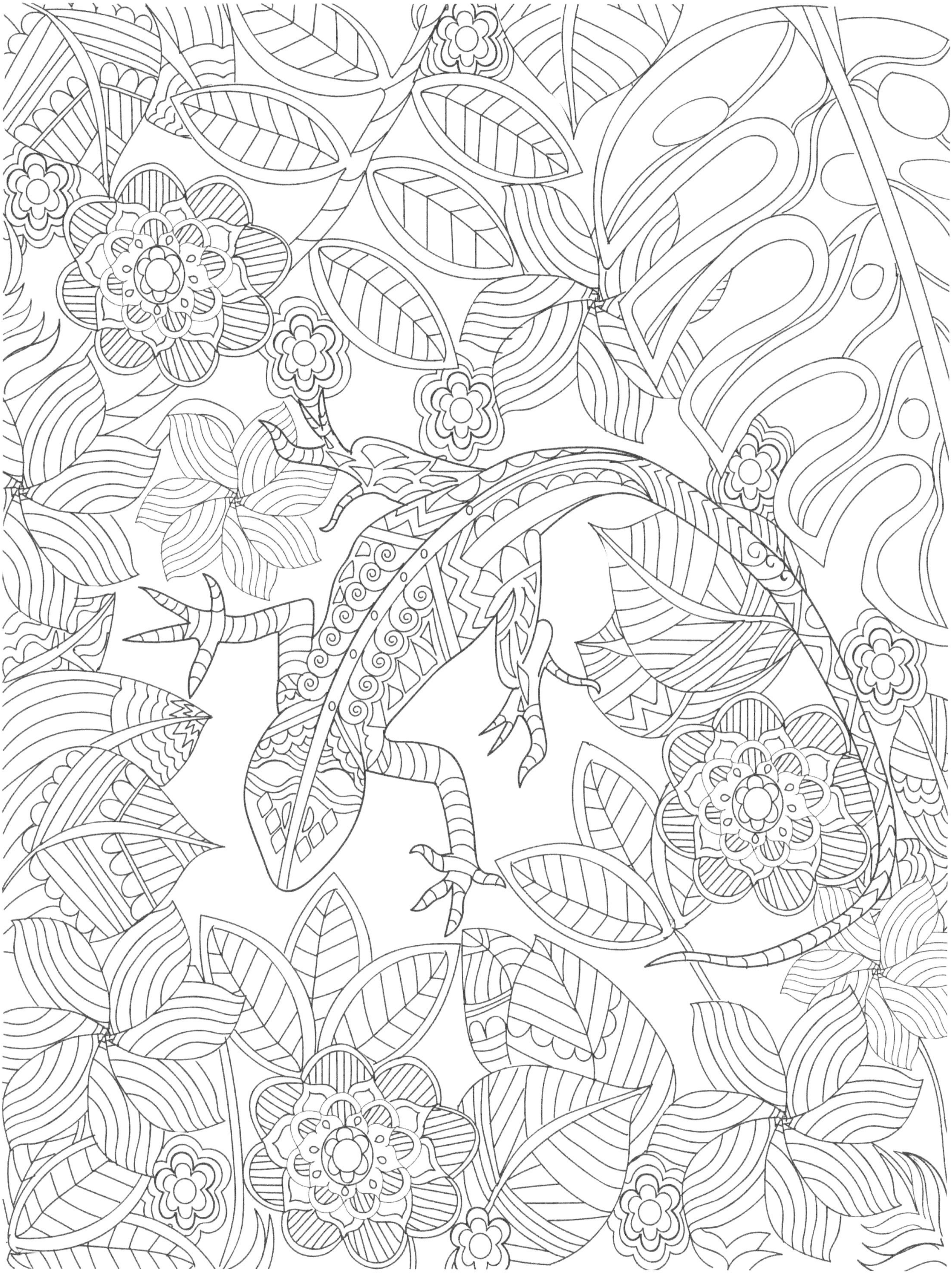

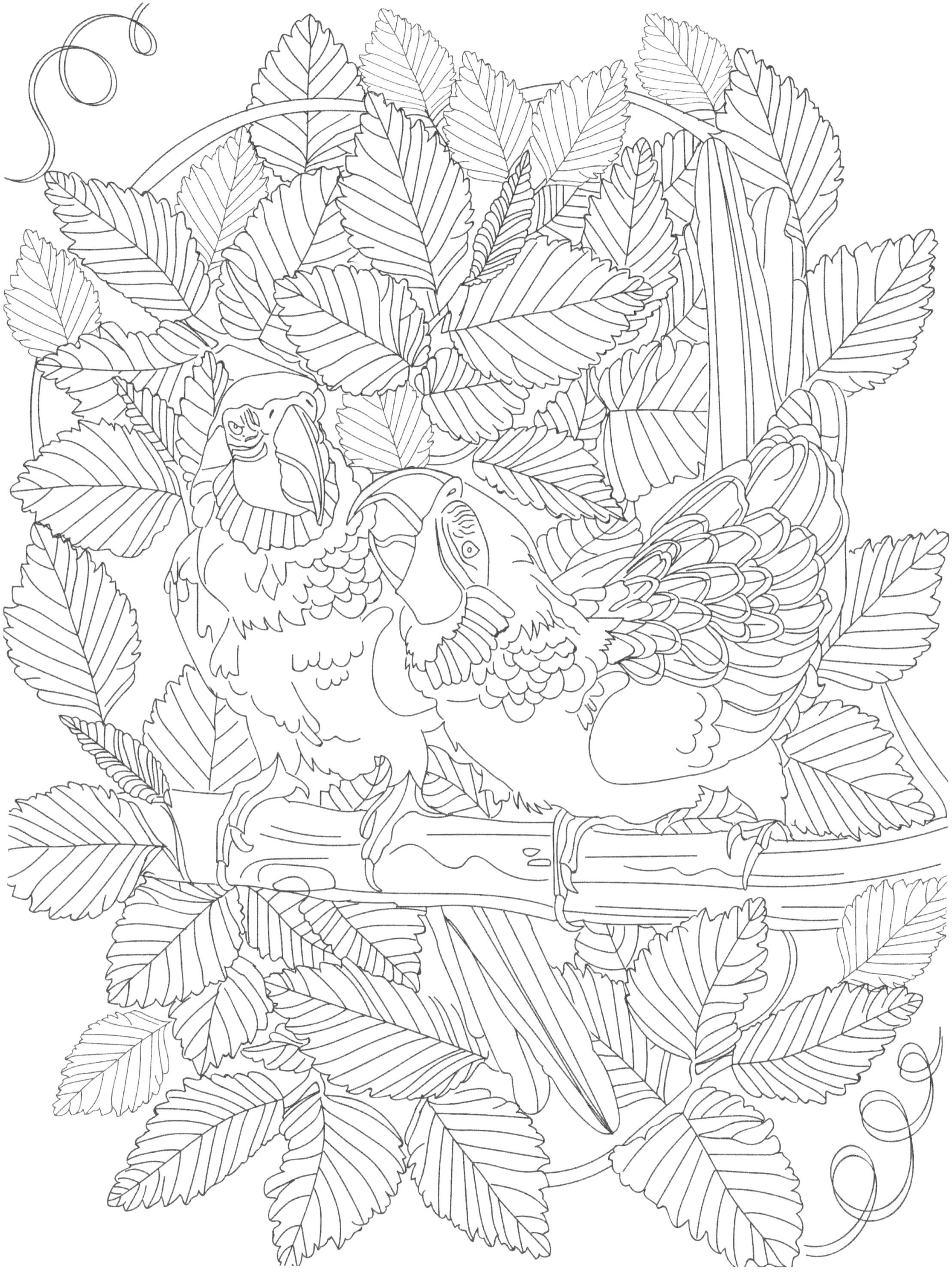

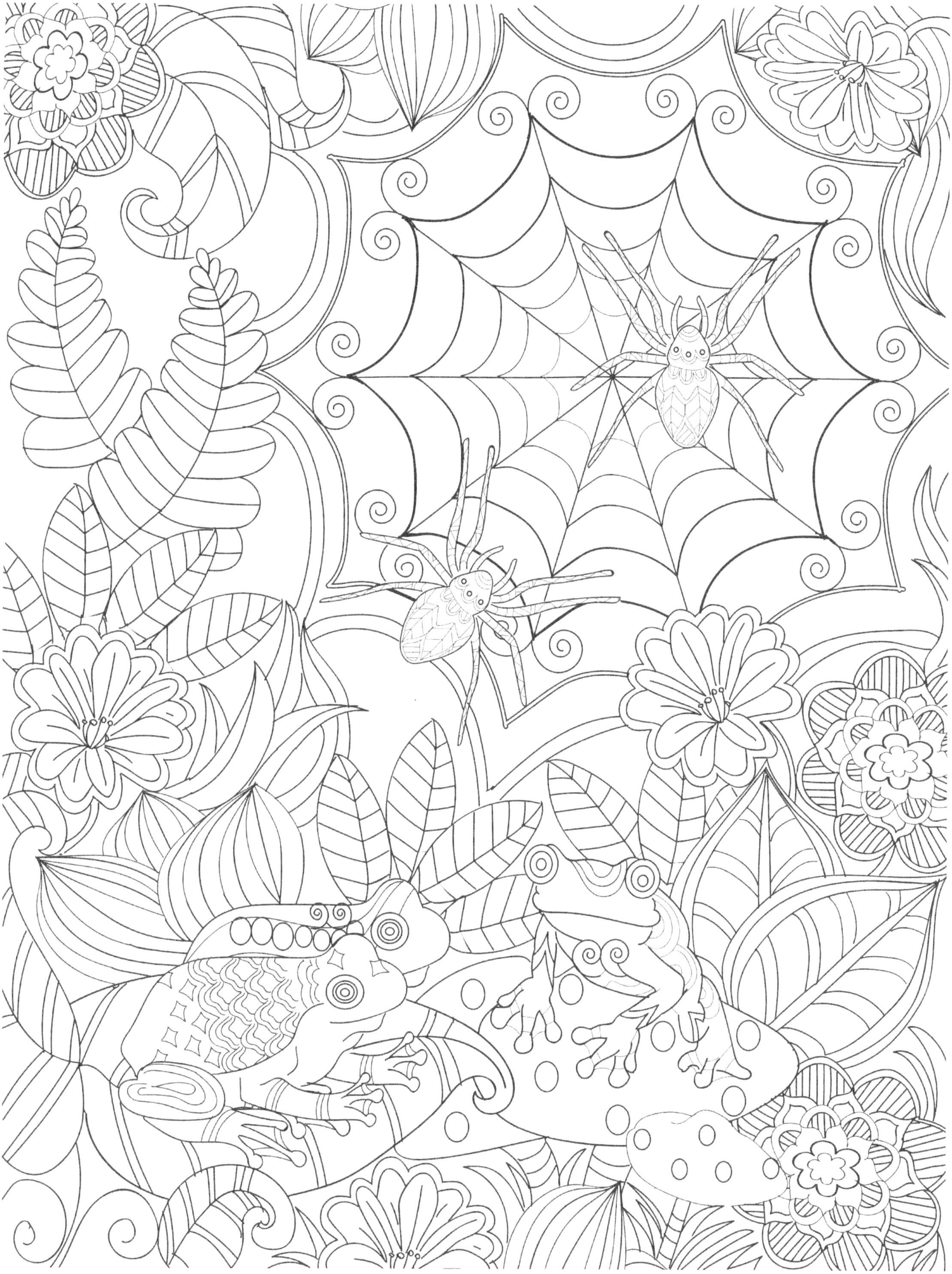

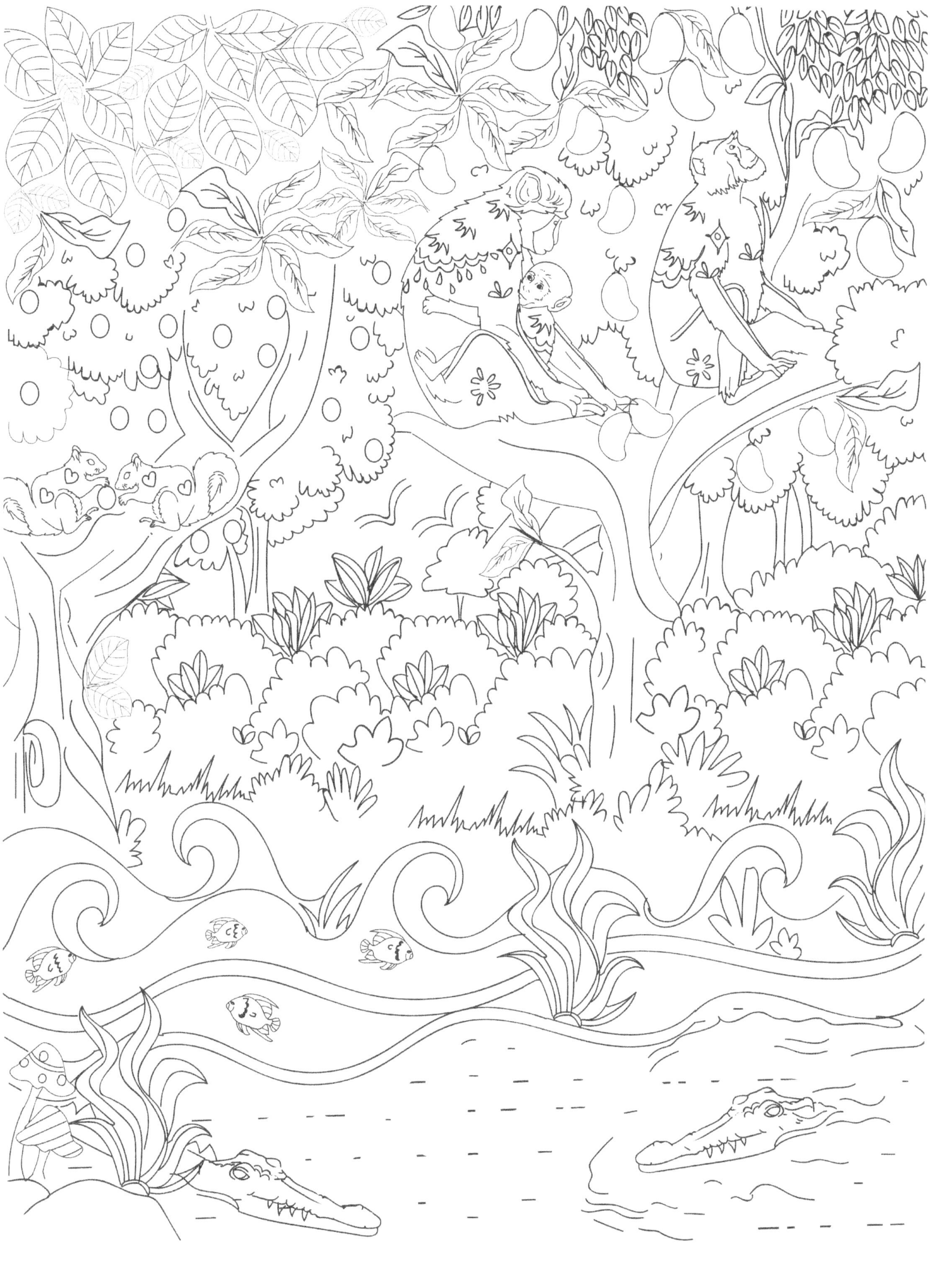

Be one of the In Crowd!

As a Mix Books Coloring Insider, you will receive FREE coloring pages to download and be among the first to know about special offers and our newest coloring books.

Sign up now, and as our thanks to you, immediately receive TEN illustrations in PDF format. Go to:

http://www.mix-booksonline.com/coloring

Other coloring books for you to enjoy:

In an Octopus's Garden: Stress Releiving Patterns
Paisley and Patterns: Intricate Designs Coloring Book
Coloring Book for Adults: BadASS Buttocks
Coloring Book of Vintage Caricatures and Characters
Silesian Folk Tales Coloring Book: Intricate Vintage Illustrations
Coloring Book for Kids: Farm Animals
Coloring Book for Kids: Monsters
Adult Coloring Book for Relaxation: Serenity: Spirit Guides & Totems
Adult Coloring Book: Stress Relief and Relaxation: Original Hand-drawn Designs
Stress Relief Coloring Book: Patterns & Designs (Adult Coloring Books)
My Heart, My Valentine & the Color of Love: Adult Coloring Book
Adult Coloring Book: Flower Designs: Stress Relieving Patterns

Easily access all of our coloring books here:

http://www.mix-booksonline.com/category/coloring-books

www.ingramcontent.com/pod-product-compliance
Lightning Source LLC
Chambersburg PA
CBHW080542190526
45169CB00007B/2597
9781533610027